FAITH CLINIC

VOLUME XXIV
-UNSEEN, NOT UNLOVED EDITION –
Discovering Purpose When You Feel Invisible

DR. PATRICIA S. TANNER

©Copyright 2026

IBG Publications, Inc.

Published by I.B.G. Publications, Inc., a Power to Wealth Company

Web address: www.ibgpublications.com

admin@ibgpublications.com / 904-419-9810

Copyright, 2026 by Patricia S. Tanner

IBG Publications, Inc., Jacksonville, FL

ISBN: 978-1-971850-10-8

Tanner, Patricia S.

Faith Clinic, Volume XXIV Unseen, Not Unloved Edition-Discovering Purpose When You Feel Invisible

---

All rights reserved. This book, or its parts may not be reproduced in any form, stored in a retrieval system, or transmitted in any form, by any means-electronic, mechanical, photocopy, recording or otherwise, without prior written permission of the publisher or author, except as provided by the United States of America Copyright law.

Printed in the United States of America.

DEDICATION

To the ones who showed up faithfully and were still overlooked. To the quiet carriers, the dependable, the consistent, the strong, who learned how to hold everything together while no one stopped to ask how you were doing.

This book is dedicated to you.

To every heart that felt invisible in rooms where you gave your best… and still felt unseen. May these pages remind you that your presence was never unnoticed by God, your obedience was never wasted, and your worth was never tied to who acknowledged it.

You were never invisible.
You were always seen, by the One who matters most.

With compassion,
DR. PATRICIA S. TANNER
The Faith Doctor

ACKNOWLEDGMENTS

To my Great Physician, Dr. Jesus, thank You for writing every chapter before I lived it. For refusing to let me self-diagnose my pain or medicate my pride. For calling me back when I mistook control for courage, and independence for identity.

To the Holy Spirit, my Counselor and Care Partner, thank You for every whisper, every nudge, every quiet correction that shaped these pages into healing. You are the steady voice in my chaos.

To my family, thank you for loving me through every rewrite, every late night, and every emotional ICU moment of this book's creation. You are my first ministry and my forever reminder that healing is a group project.

To every reader who's ever walked through their own faith rehab, thank you for showing up to your own recovery. You are proof that God still specializes in stubborn patients.

And finally, to every woman and man who's ever looked in the mirror and said, "I shouldn't still be here"… You're right, but grace decided otherwise.

TABLE OF CONTENTS

Welcome To The Clinic

If you are reading this, chances are you didn't arrive here because life collapsed loudly. You didn't have a public breakdown, a dramatic scandal, or a moment that forced people to stop and notice your pain. Your struggle has been quieter than that. It has lived in the background of rooms where you were present but not acknowledged, faithful but not affirmed, needed but not truly seen. You showed up. You carried weight. You stayed consistent. And somehow, in all that obedience, you still learned what it feels like to be invisible.

This clinic is not for people who want attention. It is for people who never asked for it and quietly paid the price for that humility. It is for the ones who learned early on how to make themselves smaller so others could feel more comfortable, more important, more secure. It is for those who were praised for being strong but never asked how much that strength cost them. It is for the dependable, the loyal, the always-there people who became so reliable that their humanity stopped being noticed.

Let's name something right away so you don't gaslight yourself as you read: invisibility hurts. Not because you need applause, but because you were created to be known. God did not design you to be useful but unseen, faithful but forgotten, present but overlooked. When you spend too long in environments where your presence is assumed and your absence is never imagined, something begins to fracture inside you. You don't always recognize it as pain at first. It feels more like numbness. Withdrawal. A quiet resignation that says, "This is just how it is."

This clinic exists because that lie has gone unchallenged for too long. Unseen does not mean unloved. But being unseen can distort how loved you believe you are. When people consistently overlook you, your heart starts to fill in the gaps with assumptions God never made. You begin to wonder if maybe you are too quiet, too ordinary, too replaceable to matter deeply. You reply to moments where you hoped someone would notice, acknowledge, affirm, or simply say thank you, and they didn't. Over time, you stop hoping. Not because you healed, but because hoping felt too expensive.

In the Faith Clinic, we don't rush past that. We don't spiritualize it with platitudes. We don't tell you to "just be grateful" or "serve harder" or "wait your turn." We slow down and examine the wound honestly, because healing requires truth before it ever produces peace. This book is not here to make you louder or more visible for the sake of people. It is here to help you reclaim your sense of worth, purpose, and identity even if the room never claps.

You need to hear this clearly at the beginning: God has never missed you. Not once. Not in the seasons where you felt forgotten. Not in the moments where your obedience went unnoticed. Not in the years when you felt like a background character in someone else's calling. Divine sight does not function like human attention. God does not overlook quietly faithful people; He often hides them intentionally. Not to punish them, but to prepare them without pressure, distortion, or performance. Still, preparation does not mean pain was imaginary. It means pain had purpose, and that purpose is now being revealed.

This clinic is where we stop confusing invisibility with insignificance. It is where we treat the quiet grief of being taken for granted. It is where we name the exhaustion that comes from always being the strong one. It is where we dismantle the fact that if you were more impressive, louder, or easier to market, you would finally be worthy of being seen. You were worthy before anyone noticed. You were loved before anyone affirmed it. And you mattered even when nobody said it out loud.

As you move through these pages, you may feel emotions surface that you learned to bury to survive. You may recognize patterns of self-erasure, over-functioning, emotional withdrawal, or spiritual burnout that you never labeled before. That is not regression. That is diagnosis. And diagnosis is the beginning of healing.

So, take a breath. You are not late. You are not dramatic. You are not asking for too much. You are finally telling the truth about what it costs to be unseen. And in this clinic, truth is not punished.

Welcome to the Faith Clinic. You are unseen no longer.

FAITH CLINIC: INTAKE FORM

Patient Diagnosis: Invisibility Trauma
Unseen, Not Unloved: Discovering Purpose When You Feel Invisible

Welcome.
This intake form is not a test, a performance review, or a place to impress God. It is a mirror. Answer honestly. No one is grading your strength.

PATIENT INFORMATION

Name (or the name you answer when no one's looking):
Date of Admission: ______________________________
Season of Life You're Currently In:
☐ Waiting
☐ Serving
☐ Surviving
☐ Burned out but still showing up
☐ Quietly questioning everything
☐ Other: ______________________________

PRIMARY COMPLAINT (Why You Came In Today)

Check all that apply:
☐ I feel invisible even when I'm present
☐ I'm relied on but rarely acknowledged
☐ I don't feel chosen, just convenient
☐ I'm tired of being "the strong one"
☐ I've stopped expecting to be seen
☐ I feel guilty for wanting affirmation
☐ I serve faithfully but feel emotionally empty

☐ I don't know if I matter outside of what I do
☐ Other (be honest): ___________________________

SYMPTOM ASSESSMENT

In the past 6–12 months, how often have you experienced the following?

Feeling emotionally unseen or overlooked:
☐ Rarely ☐ Sometimes ☐ Often ☐ Constantly
Feeling noticed only when something needs to be done:
☐ Rarely ☐ Sometimes ☐ Often ☐ Constantly
Shrinking your needs so you don't burden others:
☐ Rarely ☐ Sometimes ☐ Often ☐ Constantly
Serving while quietly resenting the lack of acknowledgment:
☐ Rarely ☐ Sometimes ☐ Often ☐ Constantly
Convincing yourself "this is just how it's supposed to be":
☐ Rarely ☐ Sometimes ☐ Often ☐ Constantly

HISTORY OF INVISIBILITY

Answer in full sentences if possible. No rushing.

1. **When was the first time you remember feeling unseen?** (Childhood, ministry, family, relationships, workplace, church, etc.)

____
____
____

2. **Who benefits most from you staying quiet, agreeable, or unnoticed?**

____
____
____

3. What parts of yourself have you learned to hide to remain accepted?

____

____

____

COPING MECHANISMS
(How You've Learned To Survive)

Check all that apply:

☐ Over-functioning (doing more so I'll matter)

☐ Emotional withdrawal ("I don't need anyone")

☐ Hyper-independence

☐ Humor to deflect pain

☐ Spiritualizing neglect ("God sees me, so it's fine")

☐ Numbing (busyness, scrolling, sleep, avoidance)

☐ Quiet resentment

☐ Self-blame

☐ Other: _______________________________

SPIRITUAL IMPACT REVIEW

Answer honestly, there are no wrong answers here.

1. My relationship with God feels:

☐ Close but quiet

☐ Faithful but dry

☐ Confused

☐ Safe

☐ Distant

☐ Unchanged

☐ Other: _______________________________

2. I secretly believe God sees everyone else more clearly than He sees me:

☐ Yes ☐ Sometimes ☐ No

3. I struggle with the idea that I can be loved without being useful:

☐ Yes ☐ Sometimes ☐ No

INTERNAL BELIEF CHECK

Complete the sentences without overthinking:

- "If I were more _____________, I would finally be seen."
- "I am easiest to love when I _____________."
- "The part of me that feels most invisible is _____________."

EMOTIONAL VITALS (Rate Honestly)

On a scale of 1–10 (1 = depleted, 10 = full):

- Sense of Worth: _______
- Emotional Energy: _______
- Hope: _______
- Feeling Known: _______
- Desire to Keep Showing Up: _______

BOUNDARY SCREENING

Answer Yes or No:

☐ I say yes when I want to say no

☐ I feel guilty when I rest

☐ I feel responsible for other people's comfort

☐ I fear being seen will cost me safety

☐ I've confused humility with self-erasure

PATIENT GOALS (What You're Hoping To Heal)

Check all that apply:

☐ To believe I matter without proving it

☐ To stop shrinking myself

☐ To reconnect with purpose

☐ To heal resentment without shame

☐ To feel seen by God again

☐ To stop apologizing for existing

☐ To learn how to take up space without guilt

☐ Other: ____

CONSENT FOR TREATMENT

Please initial:

☐ _______ I consent to honest reflection

☐ _______ I consent to naming pain I minimized

☐ _______ I consent to releasing false beliefs about my worth

☐ _______ I consent to healing even if nothing changes externally

☐ _______ I consent to being seen by God before being seen by people

PHYSICIAN'S NOTE (Read Slowly)

You are not here because you are weak.
You are here because you carried too much quietly.
Your invisibility did not mean you were unloved.
It meant you survived without witnesses.

SIGNATURE

Patient Signature: ___________________________________

Date: ____

FAITH CLINIC: DIAGNOSIS REPORT

Invisible Wound: Chronic Invisibility Trauma

Unseen, Not Unloved: Discovering Purpose When You Feel Invisible

PATIENT STATUS

Condition: Real
Severity: Accumulative
Visibility: Low
Impact: High
Urgency: Long overdue

CLINICAL SUMMARY

This patient presents with a long-standing, often undiagnosed condition known as **Invisibility Trauma**. Unlike acute emotional wounds that announce themselves loudly, this injury develops quietly over time. It forms in environments where the patient is consistently present but rarely acknowledged, faithful but not affirmed, relied upon but emotionally unseen. The wound is not caused by one dramatic moment, but by repeated absence of recognition, protection, and relational reciprocity.

Invisibility Trauma is especially common among dependable individuals, caregivers, servants, leaders, intercessors, and emotionally mature people who learned early that being low maintenance kept relationships intact. Because the pain does not disrupt rooms, it is often ignored, even by the patient.

PRIMARY DIAGNOSIS

Chronic Emotional Invisibility
A condition in which a person's presence is normalized, their

needs are minimized, and their worth becomes unconsciously tied to usefulness rather than being.

SECONDARY DIAGNOSES
(Commonly Co-Occurring)

☑ Emotional Neglect (Unintentional or Systemic)

☑ Identity Diffusion (Confusing worth with function)

☑ Suppressed Grief

☑ Relational Burnout

☑ Hyper-Independence

☑ Spiritual Overcompensation

☑ Boundary Fatigue

☑ Internalized Self-Erasure

SYMPTOMS OBSERVED

- Feeling unseen even in familiar spaces
- Being acknowledged only when something is needed
- Difficulty receiving care, affirmation, or rest
- Guilt associated with wanting to be noticed
- Emotional withdrawal disguised as maturity
- Chronic fatigue without clear cause
- Shrinking desires to avoid disappointment
- Over-functioning paired with resentment
- Silence mistaken for strength

PATIENT SELF-REPORT

The patient may state things such as:

- "It's fine. I don't need much."
- "I'm used to it."
- "Other people have it worse."

- "God sees me, so it doesn't matter."
- "I don't want to make a big deal."

Clinical Note: These statements are not signs of healing. They are adaptive survival responses.

ETIOLOGY (HOW THIS WOUND FORMS)

This condition typically develops when the patient learns, explicitly or implicitly, that their needs are inconvenient, their emotions are secondary, or their presence is assumed rather than cherished. Over time, the patient adapts by becoming emotionally efficient, spiritually productive, and relationally quiet. The wound deepens when faith language is used to justify neglect or self-denial beyond what God ever required.

MISDIAGNOSES TO RULE OUT

- Pride
- Attention-seeking
- Ingratitude
- Weak faith
- Emotional immaturity

Correction: The patient is not seeking attention. The patient is seeking acknowledgment of existence.

PROGNOSIS

Excellent, with treatment. Healing is not dependent on external validation, public recognition, or relational reversal. Recovery begins internally with truth, boundaries, and divine affirmation. While visibility from people may or may not increase, internal wholeness and spiritual stability will.

TREATMENT PRIORITIES

1. Naming the wound without minimizing it
2. Separating identity from usefulness
3. Addressing suppressed grief
4. Relearning how to receive
5. Establishing boundaries without guilt
6. Restoring internal worth independent of recognition
7. Reconnecting purpose to obedience, not applause

PHYSICIAN'S WARNING

Untreated Invisibility Trauma may lead to:
- Emotional numbness
- Resentment toward God or others
- Sudden withdrawal from community
- Burnout masked as faithfulness
- Loss of joy without loss of belief

PHYSICIAN'S AFFIRMATION

This wound was invisible, but it was never imaginary.
You did not fail to feel it.
You adapted to survive it.
Now you are allowed to heal it.

OFFICIAL DIAGNOSIS STATEMENT

The patient is not forgotten.
The patient is not insignificant.
The patient is not unloved.
The patient has been unseen and is now under care.

Attending Physician:
Faithful Presence, M.D.

⊟ FAITH CLINIC:
EMERGENCY WALLET CARD

"God Sees Me. Period." *(Carry this for moments when invisibility tries to rewrite the truth.)*

FRONT OF CARD

EMERGENCY IDENTITY STATEMENT
GOD SEES ME. PERIOD.
Not when I perform.
Not when I prove.
Not when I'm useful.
Not when someone finally notices.
He sees me **now**.

BACK OF CARD

USE IN CASE OF:
- Feeling overlooked
- Being taken for granted
- Emotional shutdown
- Serving without affirmation
- Questioning if you matter
- Shrinking to stay safe

IMMEDIATE INTERVENTION STEPS

1. **Pause.** Do not explain yourself.
2. **Breathe.** Inhale truth. Exhale the lie.
3. **Read aloud:** *"I am seen by God even if no one acknowledges me."*

TRUTH OVERRIDE

- My worth is not tied to visibility.
- My obedience still counts in silence.
- I do not disappear when I am ignored.
- God has never overlooked me.

SCRIPTURAL REMINDER

"You are the God who sees me." **Genesis 16:13**

RELAPSE WARNING

If you begin:
- Over-functioning to be noticed
- Apologizing for needing rest
- Withdrawing emotionally
- Resenting silently

Return to this card immediately.

DISCHARGE INSTRUCTION

You are not invisible.
You are not forgotten.
You are not unloved.
God sees you. Period.

INTRODUCTION

Discovering Purpose When You Feel Invisible

There is a specific kind of pain that does not announce itself. It does not crash into your life with noise or spectacle. It does not demand immediate attention or leave obvious scars. It settles quietly. It takes up residence in the spaces where you expected to be noticed but weren't, where you showed up fully and were still overlooked, where your presence became assumed instead of appreciated. This is the pain of invisibility, and it is far more common than people admit.

This book is not for people who crave the spotlight. It is for the ones who learned to live without it. It is for those who discovered early how to be dependable, quiet, agreeable, and strong, and were rewarded with being overlooked rather than honored. It is for the ones who were told they were "low maintenance," "easy," or "so strong," without anyone stopping to ask what it cost them to become that way. You didn't disappear because you wanted to. You disappeared because you adapted.

Invisibility doesn't always come from rejection. Sometimes it comes from usefulness. When people learn they can rely on you without checking on you, something subtle shifts. You are no longer asked how you are doing, because the assumption is that you're fine. You are no longer affirmed, because your consistency makes your effort invisible. You become essential but unseen, necessary but unnoticed. And over time, that dynamic teaches you something dangerous: that your value is tied to what you provide, not who you are. This is where faith complicates things.

Many people who feel invisible are deeply faithful. They serve. They pray. They show up. They obey even when no one is watching. And when the ache of being unseen begins to surface, they often silence it with spiritual language. "God sees me." "I'm serving for Him, not people." "I shouldn't need recognition." Those statements are not untrue, but they are often used to avoid naming real pain. Faith was never meant to anesthetize wounds. It was meant to heal them.

Unseen does not mean unloved. But being unseen for too long can distort how loved you believe you are. When people repeatedly overlook you, your mind starts filling in the gaps. Maybe you're too quiet. Too ordinary. Too replaceable. Maybe if you were louder, more impressive, more visible, you would finally matter. These conclusions feel logical, but they are lies formed in silence, not truth spoken by God. This book exists to interrupt that internal narrative.

Unseen, Not Unloved is not about teaching you how to be noticed. It is about helping you heal from places where not being noticed changed how you see yourself. It is about separating your identity from your usefulness, your worth from your output, and your purpose from public affirmation. It is about learning how to take up space internally even if the room never acknowledges you externally.

You may recognize yourself in these pages in uncomfortable ways. You may realize how often you minimize your needs, how easily you justified neglect, how quickly you learned to shrink your expectations so disappointment would hurt less. You may see patterns of emotional withdrawal, quiet resentment, or spiritual burnout that you never named before. That is not weakness. That is awareness. And awareness is the beginning of healing.

This book will not rush you. It will not shame you. It will not tell you to be louder, tougher, or more grateful. It will tell you the truth, gently, clearly, and repeatedly, until it starts to settle in your bones. You matter even when no one notices. Your obedience counts even when no one affirms it. Your presence has weight even when it is overlooked.

God has never missed you. Not once. Not in the background seasons. Not in the hidden work. Not in the rooms where your name was forgotten but your contribution was assumed. Divine sight does not function like human attention. God does not overlook the faithful; He often forms them out of view.

This book is an invitation to stop measuring your worth by visibility and start rooting it in truth. It is permission to name what hurts without feeling guilty for feeling it. It is a reminder that purpose does not require an audience, and love does not require witnesses. You are not here because you are broken. You are here because you carried something quietly for too long. And now, it's time to be honest about it. Welcome to *Unseen, Not Unloved*. Healing begins here.

PERSONAL NOTES

PART I: THE SYMPTOMS

PERSONAL NOTES

Chapter 1:

"NO ONE NOTICED, SO I STOPPED EXPECTING THEM TO."

SYMPTOM: Emotional Withdrawal Disguised As Maturity

One of the earliest symptoms of invisibility trauma is not anger, bitterness, or rebellion, it is withdrawal. Not physical withdrawal, where you leave rooms or relationships, but emotional withdrawal, where you stay present while slowly detaching your expectations. This symptom rarely looks alarming. In fact, it is often praised. You stop expecting people to notice you, check on you, or affirm you, and that restraint is mistaken for strength. You tell yourself that needing less is a sign of growth, that wanting acknowledgment is childish, and that emotional independence is maturity. But what happened is simpler and far more painful: hoping became too costly, so you stopped.

This symptom develops quietly. It begins the moment you realize that being unnoticed hurts less when you don't expect anything. You don't shut down all at once. You adjust. You lower the volume of your needs. You stop initiating vulnerable conversations. You learn how to meet everyone else's expectations while quietly abandoning your own. You convince yourself that you are fine, not because you are healed, but because disappointment becomes familiar. Over time, this emotional detachment starts to feel normal. You don't miss being seen anymore, you just assume it won't happen.

As this symptom progresses, you may notice a numbness settling in. Joy feels muted. Excitement feels risky. Desire feels inconvenient. You still care, but not openly. You still serve, but without anticipation. You still believe in God, but you quietly stop believing that anyone else will truly see you. The danger is not that others fail to notice you. The danger is that you learned how to disappear emotionally while staying physically present, and you started calling that survival "peace."

TEACHING: Disappearing Was A Survival Skill, Not A Calling

What you experienced was not spiritual maturity, it was adaptation. You did not stop expecting people to notice you because God asked you to. You stopped because your environment trained you too. When recognition, care, or affirmation were inconsistent or absent, your nervous system did what it was designed to do: it protected you. It reduced hope to reduce pain. It taught you how to function without needing response. That response kept you alive emotionally, but it was never meant to become your identity.

God never called you to vanish to be faithful. Scripture does not equate holiness with emotional erasure. Jesus never praised people for disappearing. He called people out of hiding. He named them. He saw them. He acknowledged them publicly and privately. Divine love does not require you to pretend you don't want to be seen. It invites you to bring that desire into the light where it can be healed instead of shamed.

This teaching matters because when survival skills go unexamined, they turn into belief systems. You begin to believe that your needs are excessive, that your presence is optional, and that wanting acknowledgment is somehow sinful. But those beliefs were not born in truth; they were born in pain. Healing begins when you recognize that disappearing was something you learned, not something you were designed for.

You are allowed to expect care. You are allowed to want acknowledgment. You are allowed to take up space without guilt. The goal is not to demand attention, but to stop erasing yourself to feel safe. When you stop confusing silence with strength and absence with peace, you make room for deeper healing, one where you no longer must disappear to belong.

This is not a call to become louder.
It is a call to become whole.

✏ Faith Prescription: Identity Without Applause

For years, your identity may have been quietly shaped by reaction instead of truth. You learned who you were based on how little attention you required, how much you could handle, and how consistently you could perform without complaint. That version of identity is functional, but it is fragile. It collapses the moment you slow down, need help, or want something in return.

Identity without applause is not identity without worth. It is identity anchored somewhere deeper than response. This prescription calls you to detach your sense of self from external recognition and reattach it to divine truth. Not as a coping mechanism, but as a foundation. You are not the people who respond to. You are who God called, formed, and knows intimately. This does not mean you stop caring about what people think. It means their attention no longer determines your existence. It means you stop auditioning for value. It means you let your presence be enough, even when it is quiet.

Take this prescription daily: Remind yourself that silence from others does not equal absence of value. Refuse to measure your worth by reaction. Reclaim your identity as something inherent, not earned.

🧬 Spiritual Vitamin: Divine Validation

Your system has been deficient in validation, not because God withheld it, but because you stopped absorbing it. When human acknowledgment became scarce, you unconsciously learned to ignore affirmation altogether. Even divine affirmation began to feel abstract or distant.

This spiritual vitamin restores internal recognition. Divine validation is not loud, but it is constant. It does not fluctuate with performance. It does not require visibility. It does not depend on usefulness. It simply exists. Daily intake includes remembering that God's awareness of you is uninterrupted. You are not off His radar. You never were. Let that truth rebuild what invisibility eroded.

🕊 Holy Spirit Consult

The Holy Spirit gently asks: *Where did you stop expecting to be seen? What did that moment cost you emotionally? What parts of yourself did you put away for safety?* This consultation is not about judgment. It is about revelation. The Spirit does not expose wounds to shame you, but to heal you. Sit with the questions. Let the answers rise without censoring them.

🙏 Guided Prayer for the Invisible Places

"God, I bring You the parts of me that learned to disappear. I bring You the moments where I stopped expecting care because it hurt too much to hope. I confess that I confused silence with strength and absence with maturity.

Heal the places where invisibility reshaped how I see myself. Teach me how to exist fully again, without guilt, without apology, without fear. Remember me that I do not have to vanish to be faithful.
Amen."

📝 Journal Pages: Naming What Was Missed

Take time to write without minimizing or spiritualizing.
* When did I first stop expecting to be noticed?

- What did I tell myself to survive that season?

- What parts of me have I kept hidden for safety?

- What would it look like to take up space again, internally first?

There is no rush. Naming what was missed is not weakness. It is the beginning of restoration.

Chapter 2:

ALWAYS PRESENT, RARELY ACKNOWLEDGED

SYMPTOM: Chronic Over-Functioning and Emotional Neglect

One of the most common symptoms of invisibility trauma shows up as over-functioning. You become the person who always shows up, always follows through, always carries the weight without complaint. You are not asked to do more, you volunteer without being asked. You anticipate needs before they are voiced. You fill gaps automatically. And while this behavior is often praised as faithfulness or leadership, it is frequently a response to being unseen. When acknowledgment is missing, usefulness becomes the substitute for visibility.

This symptom develops slowly. First, being reliable feels meaningful. You feel needed. You feel trusted. You feel important. But over time, being needed replaces being known. People stop checking on you because you are always fine. They stop asking how you're doing because you never stop functioning. Your emotional life becomes secondary to your role. And because nothing outwardly breaks, no one notices the cost. You become essential and invisible at the same time.

As this pattern continues, emotional neglect becomes normalized. You stop expecting care because you rarely receive it. You stop sharing fatigue because it disrupts the image of strength others rely on. You begin to believe that being dependable means not needing anything in return. This is not because you don't have needs. It is because expressing them feels pointless or burdensome. Over-functioning becomes a shield, and neglect becomes familiar.

TEACHING: Reliability Without Reciprocity Erodes the Soul

God never designed relationships where one person consistently pours out without being poured into. Faithfulness was never meant to require emotional starvation. Reliability is not the same as worth, and strength is not the absence of need. When over-functioning goes unexamined, it slowly erodes your sense of identity. You begin to believe that you matter only as long as you produce, carry, or perform. And when you slow down, guilt rushes in to fill the silence. This teaching reframes reliability through the lens of health rather than holiness. Being present is not wrong. Being dependable is not sinful. But when presence becomes expected instead of appreciated, and when dependability becomes permission for neglect, something is out of alignment. God values mutuality. He honors rest. He notices the unseen cost of consistency, even when others do not.

Healing begins when you stop confusing over-functioning with obedience and start allowing yourself to receive care without shame. You are not less spiritual because you need acknowledgment. You are not weak because you want reciprocity.

You are human. And God does not ask humans to disappear emotionally to be faithful. You are allowed to rest without explanation. You are allowed to need care even when you are capable.

You are allowed to matter beyond what you provide. When reliability is rooted in identity instead of insecurity, it becomes life-giving instead of life-draining. 

When reliability becomes your identity, applause becomes the measure you pretend not to need but secretly long for. This prescription is not about demanding recognition; it is about removing recognition from the center of your worth. Identity without applause means you stop defining yourself by how consistently you show up and start defining yourself by who God says you are, even on days when you are quiet, resting, or unseen. This prescription invites you to detach your value from performance. Believing that your presence matters even when you contribute nothing. To trust that rest does not make you disposable. To remember that you were loved before you were useful.

Take this daily: I am not valuable because I am reliable. I am valuable because I exist.

🧬 Spiritual Vitamin: Divine Validation

Prolonged neglect creates a deficiency in validation. You stop absorbing affirmation because you stop expecting it. This spiritual vitamin restores internal recognition by reminding your soul that God's attention toward you has never wavered. Divine validation does not fluctuate with output. It does not require consistency. It does not diminish when you slow down. Let this truth rebuild what neglect quietly eroded.

🕊 Holy Spirit Consult

The Holy Spirit asks gently:

- ✓ When did being strong become a requirement instead of a choice?
- ✓ What have you been carrying that no one noticed?
- ✓ What would it look like to let yourself be human again?

Sit with these questions without correcting the answers.

🙏 Guided Prayer for the Unnoticed Places

"God, I bring You the places where I was always present but rarely acknowledged. I bring You the exhaustion I never named and the

resentment I felt ashamed of. I confess that I learned to disappear emotionally to survive. Heal the parts of me that equated being needed with being loved. Teach me how to receive without guilt and rest without fear. Remember that I matter even when I am not carrying everything. Amen."

📝 Journal Pages: Naming What Was Missed

Write honestly, without minimizing:

- Where have I been consistently present without being acknowledged?

____

____

____

____

- What did I stop asking for because it felt unsafe or pointless?

____

____

____

____

- How has reliability shaped my identity?

____

____

____

- What would change if I believed my presence mattered even when I did less?

Naming what was missed does not make you ungrateful. It makes you whole.

PERSONAL NOTES

Chapter 3:

OVERLOOKED DOESN'T MEAN UNQUALIFIED

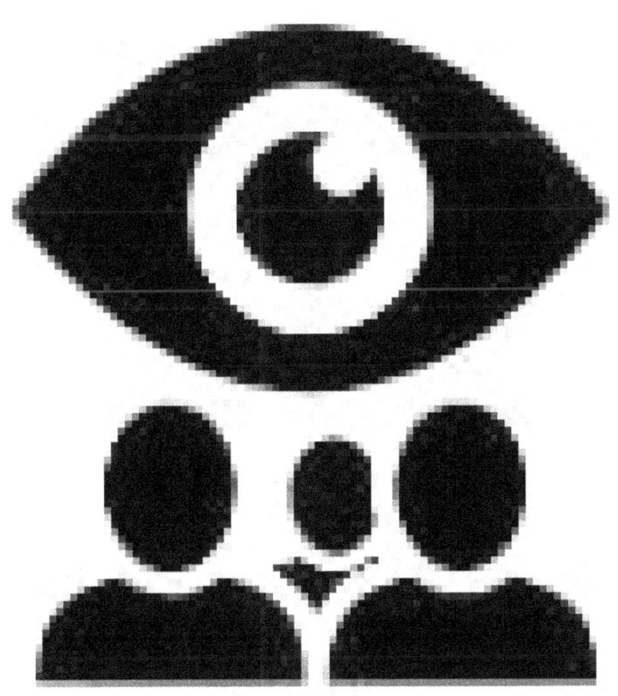

SYMPTOM: Internalized Disqualification And The Slow Erosion Of Confidence

One of the most dangerous symptoms of prolonged invisibility is not discouragement, it is internalized disqualification. This symptom does not show up as dramatic insecurity or loud self-doubt. Instead, it settles quietly into your thinking, shaping how you interpret silence, delay, and lack of recognition. You begin to assume that if you were truly capable, gifted, or called, someone would have noticed by now. And because no one has said otherwise, you let that assumption harden into belief.

This symptom forms gradually. First, you trust timing. You tell yourself, "It's not my season yet," or "God's still working things out." Those thoughts are healthy, until waiting becomes indefinite and silence becomes repetitive. Each time your name is not mentioned, your contribution is bypassed, or your voice is not invited, a subtle question forms beneath the surface: *What am I missing?* You don't ask it out loud. You ask it internally, quietly, where no one can correct it.

Over time, overlooked moments stack up. A position goes to someone else. An opportunity passes you by. A gift you carry is never acknowledged. A role you feel capable of never opens. And while none of these moments are catastrophic on their own, together they begin to rewrite how you see yourself. You stop assuming you are qualified. You start assuming you are overlooked *for a reason.* This is where the real damage happens.

Internalized disqualification does not tell you that you are worthless. It tells you that you are almost enough. Close, but not quite. Useful, but not chosen. Capable, but not exceptional. It convinces you that others must see something you don't, some hidden flaws, some missing credentials, some reason you were passed over. And because the rejection was never explicit, you cannot challenge it directly. You are left arguing with silence, and silence never explains itself.

 As this symptom deepens, it begins to affect your behavior. You hesitate before speaking, even when you know you have insight. You hold back ideas because you assume they won't be received. You stop volunteering because you don't want to feel foolish offering something no one asked for. You become cautious with your gifts, not because they are weak, but because you no longer trust that they belong in the room.

This is how invisibility trains you to self-edit.

You don't stop being gifted. You stop offering yourself freely. You start waiting for permission that never comes. And because you are faithful, you interpret that waiting as humility. You tell yourself that staying quiet is obedience, that stepping back is maturity, that not pushing forward is wisdom. But often, what you are doing is protect yourself from the pain of being overlooked again.

The tragedy of internalized disqualification is that it looks like restraint but functions like restriction. It narrows your sense of possibility. It lowers your expectations. It quietly reshapes your calling into something smaller, safer, and less visible. You begin to believe that maybe your role is simply to support others, not to lead. To assist, not to initiate. To serve, not to step forward. And while service is honorable, shrinking yourself to survive is not the same thing as obedience.

This symptom often shows up alongside comparison. You notice who is chosen. You notice who is affirmed. You notice who is visible. And without meaning to, you begin measuring yourself against outcomes rather than truth. You assume that visibility equals qualification and silence equals insufficiency. You forget that human systems reward familiarity, charisma, and timing, not always readiness or depth. But comparison rarely allows for nuance. It deals with conclusions, not context. Eventually, you may stop dreaming altogether.

Dreaming feels risky when history suggests disappointment. Hoping feels naïve when past efforts went unnoticed. You tell yourself you are content, but the contentment feels hollow. It feels more like resignation. And resignation, when left unchecked, slowly disconnects you from your sense of purpose. You still believe in God, but you stop believing in what He might do *through you*.
This is the most dangerous outcome of invisibility trauma: not that others fail to see you, but that you begin to see yourself as less than you are.

TEACHING: God's Qualification Has Never Depended On Human Recognition

God has never used visibility as a measure of readiness. From the beginning, His pattern has been consistent: He calls people long before people agree with Him. He qualifies individuals privately before He ever affirms them publicly. And He often allows long seasons of obscurity not as punishment, but as preparation. Yet when you are living in obscurity, preparation feels like neglect.

The problem is not that God's way is unclear, it is that human systems have trained us to equate affirmation with approval and silence with rejection. We are conditioned to believe that opportunity validates calling, that recognition confirms readiness, and that being overlooked must mean something is wrong. But God does not operate on consensus. He does not crowdsource calling. He does not wait for others to notice you before He assigns purpose.

 Throughout Scripture, God consistently chooses people who are overlooked by their own communities. Shepherds. Younger siblings. Outsiders. People with no platform, no title, no obvious advantage. Not because He enjoys surprising people, but because human perception is limited. God looks at posture, not popularity. He looks at obedience, not optics. He looks at faithfulness in hidden places, not performance in visible ones.

But even knowing this, the emotional weight of being overlooked is real.

God never dismisses that pain. He does not shame people for feeling unseen. What He corrects is the interpretation of silence. Silence from people is not silence from God. Delay is not denial. And being overlooked by others does not cancel divine qualifications.

One of the reasons God allows seasons of invisibility is because visibility has the power to distort identity if it comes too early. Recognition without rootedness creates fragility. Affirmation without foundation breeds insecurity. God is not withholding opportunity from you; He is protecting you from attaching your worth to response. He is ensuring that when doors open, you will walk through them knowing who you are, not needing others to tell you. Still, protection often feels like abandonment when you do not understand it.

This teaching does not ask you to romanticize waiting or pretend that being overlooked does not hurt. It asks you to reinterpret waiting correctly. Waiting is not a sign that you are behind. It is often a sign that God is working beneath the surface, strengthening what will eventually be seen. Roots grow in darkness. Foundations form underground. And nothing built to last is constructed in a hurry.

God's qualification is not fragile. It does not expire because others do not notice it. It does not diminish because opportunities have not come yet. It is established by His word, His timing, and His purpose. No amount of silence can undo what God has already spoken over you.

Healing begins when you stop using human response as a measuring stick for divine calling. When you stop interpreting silence as a verdict. When you stop assuming that being overlooked means being overlooked by God. And when you allow yourself to believe that who you are in hidden seasons matters just as much as who you will be in visible ones.

You were not overlooked because you were unqualified. You were overlooked because visibility is not the same thing as readiness. God's call on your life does not need witnesses to be valid. It only needs obedience.

🔖 Faith Prescription: Confidence Rooted In Calling, Not Confirmation

This prescription addresses the habit of looking outward for permission to believe in what God already spoke inwardly. For too long, your confidence may have been tied to response, who noticed, who affirmed, who invited, who chose. This treatment redirects your focus back to calling itself. Calling does not require consensus. It requires faith.

Take this prescription daily by reminding yourself that obedience does not need applause to be effective. You are allowed to trust what God placed inside you even if no one else has named it yet. Confidence rooted in calling is steady. It does not rise and fall with attention. It does not disappear in silence.

⚕ Spiritual Vitamin: Divine Authorization

You do not need human permission to be who God called you to be. This spiritual vitamin restores internal authorization. Gods "yes" were never dependent on a committee, a title, or a platform. Take this truth daily until it becomes louder than doubt.

🕊 Holy Spirit Consult

Ask honestly and listen quietly:
- Where have I interpreted silence as rejection?
- Where have I stopped trusting my own gifts?
- What have I been waiting for permission to do?

Let the Spirit respond without rushing to correct the answer.

🙏 Guided Prayer

"God, I confess that silence made me question myself. I allowed being overlooked to make me doubt what You placed inside me. Heal the places where I shrank instead of trusting You. Restore my confidence, not in visibility, but in obedience. Help me believe that Your calling on my life is secure, even in hidden seasons. Amen."

📝 Journal Pages: Reclaiming What Silence Tried To Steal

Write without filtering:
- Where did I assumed I was unqualified because I was overlooked?

____

____

- What gifts have I hidden out of fear of being ignored?

- What would change if I trusted God's call without waiting for validation?

You are not late. You are not lacking. You are becoming.

Chapter 4:

WHEN YOU START SHRINKING SO OTHERS FEEL COMFORTABLE

SYMPTOM: Self-Erasure Disguised As Humility

One of the most painful symptoms of invisibility trauma is not that you feel unseen by others, but that you slowly begin to make yourself smaller, so no one feels threatened, inconvenienced, or uncomfortable by your presence. This symptom rarely looks dramatic. It looks like consideration. It looks like humility. It looks like emotional intelligence. But beneath the surface, it is something far more costly: self-erasure.

Self-erasure begins as a response to environment. When you notice that your full presence makes others uneasy, overlooked, or defensive, you adapt. You soften your opinions. You dim your passion. You downplay your gifts. You shrink your voice. You do not do this because you lack confidence, but because you learned that standing out comes with consequences, misunderstanding, dismissal, isolation, or being labeled "too much." Shrinking becomes the price of belonging.

This symptom develops quietly. You learn which parts of yourself are welcome and which parts disrupt the room. You notice when your insight is ignored but your compliance is praised. You feel when your confidence shifts energy in ways people do not know how to hold. And instead of demanding space, you withdraw. You choose peace over presence. You choose safety over authenticity. You convince yourself that being less visible is wiser than being misunderstood.

Over time, this adaptation becomes automatic. You stop asking yourself what you think and start asking what will be easiest for others to hear. You filter your words before they leave your mouth. You hesitate before expressing needs. You become highly attuned to others 'comfort while growing increasingly disconnected from your own. You do not disappear entirely, you curate yourself.

This is how shrinking masquerades are as kindness. You tell yourself you are being considerate. You say you are flexible, easygoing, adaptable. And in many ways, you are. But flexibility without boundaries slowly turns into self-abandonment. When you consistently choose others 'comfort over your own expression, you teach yourself that your full self is too much to offer. You internalize the belief that your presence needs to be managed, contained, or edited to be acceptable.

As this symptom deepens, it begins to affect your sense of identity. You lose clarity about who you are because you are always adjusting to the room. You feel disoriented when asked what you want because you are more practiced at knowing what others expect. You struggle to name your desires because you learned that wanting too much makes people uncomfortable. And without realizing it, you begin to associate authenticity with risk.

This is especially common among people who are perceptive, emotionally intelligent, or spiritually sensitive. You can feel the emotional temperature of a room, and you know when your presence changes . Instead of trusting that sensitivity as a gift, you use it as a signal to retreat. You mistake your awareness for responsibility. You begin regulating yourself, so others do not have to regulate their discomfort.

Eventually, you may notice resentment forming, not toward others, but toward yourself. You feel frustrated that you cannot fully show up. You feel tired of constantly managing how you are perceived. You feel disconnected from your own voice. And yet, the idea of taking up space again feels terrifying. Shrinking has become familiar. Visibility feels unsafe. This is the hidden cost of self-erasure: you survive socially but disappear internally.

TEACHING: God Never Asked You To Make Yourself Smaller To Be Holy

God does not confuse humility with invisibility. Humility is not the absence of presence; it is the absence of arrogance. Self-erasure, on the other hand, is the absence of self. And God never asked you to lose yourself to follow Him.

Throughout Scripture, humility is expressed through obedience, teachability, and surrender, not through silence, shrinking, or self-neglect. Jesus was humble, but He was never small. He did not edit His truth to protect people's comfort. He did not dim His authority to maintain access. He did not withdraw His presence to keep the room calm. His humility was rooted in identity, not insecurity.

When you shrink to make others comfortable, you respond to fear, not faith. Fear of being misunderstood. Fear of being rejected. Fear of disrupting relational equilibrium. And while those fears are understandable, especially if you have been overlooked or dismissed before, they are not meant to lead you.

God's design for community was never built on one person carrying discomfort so everyone else can remain comfortable. Those dynamics produce imbalance, not unity. When you consistently silence yourself to maintain peace, peace becomes performative. It looks calm on the surface, but it is sustained by suppression underneath.

God invites you into a different kind of wholeness, one where your presence is not a problem to be solved but a gift to be stewarded. This teaching reframes self-expression as stewardship rather than selfishness. You are not responsible for managing other people's reactions to your authenticity. You are responsible for showing up truthfully, lovingly, and with integrity. When others feel uncomfortable around your fullness, that discomfort often reveals something they need to process, not something you need to erase.

Healing begins when you stop confusing shrinking with wisdom. Wisdom does not require disappearance. Discernment does not demand self-denial. God's calling on your life includes your voice, your insight, your perspective, and your presence. Muting those things may keep rooms comfortable, but it keeps you disconnected from yourself. God does not need you to be smaller to be holy. He needs you to be whole.

💊 Faith Prescription: Courageous Presence

This prescription calls you to practice showing up without editing yourself to fit the room. Courageous presence does not mean being loud or forceful. It means being honest. It means allowing your thoughts, needs, and convictions to exist without apology. It means trusting that God can handle the outcomes of your authenticity.

Take this prescription daily by noticing when you shrink and gently choosing not to. Allow yourself to speak one unfiltered truth at a time. Presence is not something you demand, it is something you allow.

🧬 Spiritual Vitamin: Wholeness Without Apology

This spiritual vitamin restores your permission to exist fully. God did not create extra parts of you by accident. Your sensitivity, strength, insight, and conviction are not flaws to be minimized. Take this truth daily until you no longer feel the need to dilute yourself to belong.

🕊 Holy Spirit Consult

Ask and listen:

- Where have I been shrinking to keep others comfortable?

- What parts of myself have I learned to hide?
- What would it look like to show up fully again?

Let the answers surface without judgment.

🙏 Guided Prayer

God, I confess that I learned to make myself smaller to feel safe. I silenced parts of myself to keep peace. Healing the fear that tells me my fullness is a problem. Teach me how to take up space without guilt. Restore the parts of me I put away to survive. Amen.

📝 Journal Pages: Reclaiming Your Fullness

Write honestly:

- Where do I shrink automatically?

____

____

____

- What am I afraid would happen if I showed up fully?

____

____

- What parts of me deserve to be restored?

____

____

____

You were never meant to disappear to belong. You were meant to be whole.

Chapter 5:

SERVING WHILE UNSEEN: THE BURNOUT NOBODY PRAYS FOR

SYMPTOM: Holy Burnout And The Exhaustion You're Ashamed To Admit

One of the most misunderstood symptoms of invisibility trauma is burnout that forms in the middle of faithfulness. Not rebellion. Not disengagement. Not walking away from God. But exhaustion that develops while you are still praying, still serving, still showing up, still believing. This kind of burnout is especially dangerous because it hides behind obedience. It is rarely named because it feels inappropriate to admit. After all, you are doing "good things." You are serving God. You are helping others. You are faithful. And somewhere along the way, you learned that feeling tired in holy spaces must mean something is wrong with *you*.

This symptom develops slowly, often invisibly. At first, serving feels meaningful. It gives you purpose. It gives you structure. It gives you a sense of belonging, especially if you have felt unseen elsewhere. You begin pouring yourself into roles,  responsibilities, ministries, relationships, and callings because they give your presence weight. You may not feel seen, but you feel useful, and usefulness becomes the substitute for connection.

Over time, however, the emotional cost begins to rise. You notice that you are always giving and rarely receiving. You notice that your needs are consistently postponed in the name of faithfulness. You notice that rest feels indulgent and asking for help feels like failure. But instead of slowing down, you double down. You serve harder. You pray longer. You show up more consistently. You assume that exhaustion is a spiritual problem instead of a human one.

This is how holy burnout forms. Holy burnout is not caused by too much serving. It is caused by serving while unseen, unacknowledged, and unsupported. It is what happens when spiritual output replaces emotional nourishment. You begin to feel drained, but you don't know how to stop because stopping feels disobedient. You feel empty, but you don't know how to name it because emptiness feels ungrateful. You are tired, but you tell yourself that tiredness is the price of calling.

As this symptom deepens, you may notice subtle changes. Joy feels harder to access. Compassion begins to thin. Worship feels more like obligation than intimacy. You still believe in God, but you feel disconnected from Him emotionally. Prayer becomes functional instead of relational. You talk to God about tasks instead of your heart. And because you are still outwardly faithful, no one suspects anything is wrong.

Including you.

Eventually, resentment begins to surface, not toward God necessarily, but toward the expectations placed on you. You resent being needed but not nurtured. You resent being relied on but not restored. You resent the unspoken assumption that your strength means you don't require care. And then guilt rushes in. You feel ashamed for resenting something that is supposed to be holy. You tell yourself you should be grateful for the opportunity to serve. You push your feelings down and keep going.

This is the danger of burnout in invisible people: it is sustained by silence and sanctified by faith language.

You may begin withdrawing emotionally while still being physically present. You do what is required, but without anticipation or delight. You feel numb where passion used to live. You fantasize about rest, escape, or disappearing, not because you want to abandon God, but because you are desperate for relief. And yet, the idea of stepping back feels impossible. You don't know who you would be without what you do.

This is where burnout becomes identity threatening.

You are no longer just tired. You are afraid. Afraid that if you stop serving, you will stop mattering. Afraid that if you rest, you will be forgotten. Afraid that your value will disappear if your output does. So, you keep going, not because you are called to, but because you are terrified of what will happen if you don't. This is not devotion. This is survival.

TEACHING: God Never Asked You To Bleed Quietly On The Altar

God does not require exhaustion as proof of obedience. He does not equate depletion with devotion. And He does not confuse burnout with sacrifice. Somewhere along the way, many faithful people absorbed the belief that serving God means emptying themselves until nothing is left. But that belief is not biblical. It is broken.

True sacrifice in Scripture is never disconnected from care. God consistently commands rest, rhythm, and restoration, not as rewards for obedience, but as requirements for sustainability. Even Jesus withdrew. Even Jesus rested. Even Jesus stepped away from crowds, demands, and expectations. Not because He was weak, but because He was whole.

Burnout is not a sign that you love God deeply. It is often a sign that boundaries were ignored, needs were dismissed, and identity became tangled with output.

When you serve while unseen, you begin confusing usefulness with worth. You assume that God values you most when you are productive. You forget that before you ever did anything for Him, He called you beloved. Service was never meant to replace relationships. Ministry was never meant to consume humanity. Obedience was never meant to erase personhood. God does not ask you to destroy yourself to prove loyalty.

This teaching invites you to disentangle holiness from exhaustion. To recognize that burnout is not a spiritual badge of honor, but a warning light. It is your soul signaling that something is out of alignment. That you have been giving without receiving. That you have been pouring without being replenished. That you have been faithful to systems and expectations that did not return care.

Healing begins when you allow yourself to believe that God values you beyond your service. That rest is not rebellion. That stepping back is not failure. That being unseen does not mean you must overperform to stay worthy.

God does not need you drained to be glorified. He needs you whole. When you stop serving from fear and start serving from fullness, everything changes. Service becomes an overflow, not a transaction. Obedience becomes life-giving again. And faith stops feeling like something you survive and starts feeling like something you live.

💊 Faith Prescription: Serving From Fullness, Not Fear

This prescription addresses the belief that rest threatens your worth. Serving from fullness means you stop using exhaustion as evidence of faithfulness. It means you give from overflow, not obligation. It means you learn to pause without panic and rest without guilt. Take this prescription daily by asking yourself one question before you say yes: *Am I serving from love, or from fear of disappearing?*

🧬 Spiritual Vitamin: Rest as Divine Permission

This spiritual vitamin restores your permission to stop. God's approval does not increase when you exhaust yourself. Rest is not something you earn after burnout, it is something God designed to protect you from it. Take this truth daily until rest no longer feels like rebellion.

🕊 Holy Spirit Consult

Ask honestly:

- Where am I serving without being nourished?
- What am I afraid it would happen if I rested?
- How has service replaced intimacy with God?

Listen without defending yourself.

🙏 Guided Prayer

"God, I confess that I served until I was empty. I believed exhaustion meant obedience. Heal the places where I bled quietly and called it faithfulness. Teach me how to rest without guilt. Restore joy where duty replaced delight. Amen."

📝 Journal Pages: Reclaiming Sacred Rest

Write without minimizing:

- Where am I burned out but still showing up?

____

____

____

____

- What have I been afraid to stop doing?

____

____

____

____

- Who am I if my worth is not tied to my service?

____

____

____

____

You were never meant to disappear on the altar. You were meant to live.

PERSONAL NOTES

PART II: THE DIAGNOSIS

PERSONAL NOTES

62

Chapter 6:
WHEN SILENCE BECOMES SELF-INTERPRETATION

SYMPTOM: Meaning-Making In The Absence Of Answers

 One of the most subtle and destructive symptoms of invisibility trauma is what happens when silence goes unanswered for too long. Not just silence from people, but silence from explanations. Silence from clarity. Silence from reassurance. When no one names what's happening, your mind does what it was designed to do: it fills in the gaps. Unfortunately, it rarely fills them with truth.

This symptom does not begin as self-hatred. It begins as curiosity. *Why didn't they respond? Why wasn't I included? Why didn't anyone check on me? Why does it feel like I'm always on the outside looking in?* First, these questions feel reasonable. Healthy, even. You assume there is a logical explanation. Timing. Oversight. Busyness. You tell yourself not to take it personally.

But when silence repeats itself, curiosity turns into interpretation. When no one explains the absence, your mind creates a story. And that story almost always centers you on as the problem. You assume you missed something. You assume you misunderstood your value. You assume you are less wanted than you thought. Silence becomes evidence. Not real evidence, but emotional evidence, and emotional evidence is powerful.

This is where invisibility becomes internalized. Instead of asking others for clarity, you start answering yourself. *They didn't respond because I don't matter. They didn't invite me because I'm not important. They didn't check on me because they assumed I wouldn't need it.* Each unanswered moment becomes a data point, and eventually, those data points form a belief system.

The most dangerous part of this symptom is that it feels rational. You are not spiraling. You are observing patterns. You are connecting dots. You are making sense of your experience. But the dots you are connecting are incomplete, and the story you are telling yourself is missing truth. Silence is not confirmation, but it feels like one when it happens often enough.

As this symptom deepens, you begin adjusting your behavior based on assumptions instead of facts. You stop reaching out because you assume it won't be reciprocated. You stop sharing honestly because you assume it won't be received. You stop expressing disappointment because you assume it won't matter. You quietly accept invisibility as reality rather than circumstance.

This is how silence trains you to self-abandon. You no longer wait for others to dismiss you; you preemptively dismiss yourself. You interpret lack of response as lack of interest. You interpret absence of affirmation as absence of worth. And because no one corrects those interpretations, they begin to feel true. Over time, you stop questioning them.

This symptom often produces hyper-awareness. You read into tone. You analyze timing. You overthink interactions. You reply to conversations, looking for clues. Not because you are insecure, but because you are trying to protect yourself from future disappointment. You are trying to predict pain so it hurts less when it arrives.

But predictions based on incomplete information always leads to distortion. Eventually, this symptom begins to affect how you hear God as well. Silence in prayer starts to feel personal. Waiting seasons feel punitive. Delay begins to feel like disapproval. You may still believe in God, but you start if His silence means something negative about xyou. That you missed Him. That you misunderstood His promises. That you are less favored than others. This is not faithlessness. This is wounded interpretation.

TEACHING: Silence Is Not A Verdict, It Is An Invitation To Truth

Silence has never meant what wounded minds assume it means. In Scripture, silence is rarely punished and almost never rejected. It is often space. Space for formation. Space for trust. Space for growth cannot happen when everything is explained.

 God's silence is not absence. And human silence is not always intentional.

One of the greatest dangers of invisibility trauma is assuming that silence speaks clearly when it does not. Silence is ambiguous by nature. It requires interpretation. And when interpretation is shaped by pain instead of truth, it leads you away from reality rather than toward it.

God never invites you to interpret silence alone. Throughout Scripture, God repeatedly warns against leaning on understanding shaped by fear or insecurity. He invites trust not because questions are wrong, but because conclusions formed without Him are unreliable. Silence is meant to draw you closer, not push you inward. It is meant to lead you to seek truth, not assume lies.

When God is silent, He is not withholding affection. He is often deepening foundation. When people are silent, it is not always a statement about your worth. Sometimes it is about their limitations, distractions, immaturity, or blind spots. But invisibility trauma trains you to personalize everything, because personalizing gives you a sense of control, even if that control hurts. God wants to heal that pattern.

This teaching reframes silence as a place of inquiry rather than accusation. Instead of asking, *What's wrong with me?* you are invited to ask, *What is true here?* Instead of assuming disqualification, you are invited to seek clarity. Instead of filling gaps with self-blame, you are invited to fill them with God's voice. Healing begins when you stop letting silence narrate your worth. You are not responsible for interpreting every absence. You are not required to make sense of every unanswered moment. And you are not meant to carry conclusions that God never spoke. Silence does not cancel calling. Delay does not erase love. Waiting does not mean you failed. God's truth is always louder than silence, when you stop filling the quiet with lies.

🔎 Faith Prescription: Truth Over Assumptions

This prescription addresses the habit of filling silence with self-criticism. Instead of assuming meaning, you are invited to pause and ask God what is true. Truth over assumptions requires humility, not the humility of shrinking, but the humility of admitting you do not know everything. Take this prescription daily by interrupting assumptions as soon as they form. Replace "They didn't because I'm not enough" with "I do not have enough information to decide my worth."

🧬 Spiritual Vitamin: Divine Interpretation

You were never meant to interpret silence on your own. This spiritual vitamin restores trust in God's ability to clarify what silence obscures. Ask Him to interpret moments you don't understand instead of punishing yourself for them.

🕊 Holy Spirit Consult

Ask and wait:
- Where have I assumed the worst without evidence?
- What silence have I personalized unnecessarily?
- What truth am I avoiding because assumption feels safer?

Listen gently.

🙏 Guided Prayer

"God, I confess that silence made me turn against myself. I filled unanswered moments with conclusions You never spoke. Heal my mind where assumption replaced truth. Teach me how to wait without self-blame. Remember that silence is not rejection. Amen."

📝 Journal Pages: Rewriting The Story Silence Told

Write freely:

- What silence have I interpreted as rejection?

____

____

____

- What story did I tell myself about it?

____

____

____

- What alternative truths could also be possible?

____

____

____

Silence is not your enemy. The lies you learned to tell yourself in it are.

Chapter 7:

YOU LEARNED TO BE INVISIBLE TO STAY SAFE

SYMPTOM: Safety-Based Identity And The Fear Of Being Fully Seen

One of the most deeply rooted symptoms of invisibility trauma is  not a desire to disappear, it is the belief that being fully seen is unsafe. This symptom does not come from weakness or lack of confidence. It comes from experience. At some point, you learned, consciously or unconsciously, that visibility came with consequences. Being noticed meant being criticized, misunderstood, burdened, corrected, dismissed, or expected to carry more than you could hold. So, your system adapted. You didn't stop existing. You stopped *exposing* yourself.

This symptom forms early and quietly. It often begins in environments where emotional expression was inconvenient, honesty was punished, or presence was conditional. You noticed what happened when you spoke too much, needed too much, felt too deeply, or stood out too clearly. Maybe you were labeled dramatic. Maybe you were ignored. Maybe you were corrected instead of comforted. Maybe your vulnerability was used against you. Whatever the cause, your nervous system learned a simple rule: *visibility equals risk.*

And so, invisibility became safety.

You learned how to read rooms. You learned when to soften your voice, when to withhold emotion, when to stay neutral, when to fade into the background. You learned how to be agreeable, helpful, quiet, and non-threatening. You learned how to survive by being easy to overlook. And because these strategies worked, they reduced conflict, disappointment, and pain, you kept them.

The problem is that what keeps you safe in one season can imprison you in the next.

As this symptom deepens, invisibility stops being something you *do* and starts becoming something you *are.* You no longer consciously choose to stay hidden; you default to it. You hesitate before sharing. You feel exposed when attention turns toward you. You downplay achievements. You deflect praise. You feel uneasy when someone asks about you in depth. Being seen feels intrusive, even when it is kind. This is not humility. This is fear-based self-protection.

Over time, this symptom begins shaping identity. You stop knowing who you are outside of survival. You feel safer being needed than being known. You feel more comfortable being helpful than being honest. You are skilled at presence without vulnerability, engagement without exposure, connection without risk. And while this keeps you emotionally protected, it also keeps you emotionally alone.

The most painful part of this symptom is that it creates internal conflict. You want to be known, but you don't trust it. You desire connection, but you fear the cost. You crave acknowledgment, but visibility feels dangerous. So, you exist in a constant state of tension, longing for what you are afraid to receive.

This symptom often shows up as anxiety when attention turns toward you. Compliments feel uncomfortable. Invitations feel threatening. Opportunities feel heavy. You may feel overwhelmed by being chosen, spotlighted, or affirmed not because you don't want it, but because you don't know how to exist safely inside it. Your system learned invisibility, not integration.

Eventually, safety-based identity limits growth. You avoid opportunities that require visibility. You resist stepping forward even when invited. You talk yourself out of things you are capable of. You tell yourself you prefer being behind the scenes. And while that may be true for some, for others it is a trauma response masquerading as preference. You confuse what feels familiar with what is healthy. Invisibility kept you safe once. But now it is costing you fullness.

TEACHING: God Is Not Threatened By Your Visibility

God never designed safety to come from disappearance. He designed safety to come from *belonging*. And belonging does not require you to be hidden; it requires you to be held. Somewhere along the way, safety became synonymous with silence for you. But God does not protect you by erasing you. He protects you by surrounding you with truth, presence, and care.

Throughout Scripture, God consistently calls people out of hiding, not to expose them, but to heal them. From Adam in the garden to Elijah in the cave, God does not punish hiding; He addresses it. He asks questions not to shame, but to invite honesty. Visibility in God's hands is not threat; it is restoration.

This teaching reframes visibility as something God shepherds, not something you endure alone. Being seen by God is not invasive. It is intimate. It is gentle. It is protective. God does not spotlight you to harm you. He brings you into the light so you no longer must protect yourself.

Fear-based identity develops when protection becomes self-managed. You learned to keep yourself safe because you didn't trust others to do it. But God does not ask you to manage your own safety through disappearance. He asks you to trust Him with your visibility, one step at a time.

Healing does not mean instant exposure. It means gradual safety-building. It means allowing yourself to be seen in environments where you are honored, not exploited. It means relearning that attention does not always lead to harm. It means disentangling past pain from present possibility. God is not asking you to be reckless with your heart. He is asking you to stop hiding it from Him.

Visibility does not erase wisdom. Being seen does not cancel boundaries. And stepping forward does not mean stepping unprotected. God's presence goes with you into visibility. He does not send you there alone.

💊 Faith Prescription: Safe Visibility

This prescription invites you to practice being seen in small, safe ways. Not for performance. Not for approval. But for integration. Safe visibility means allowing yourself to exist fully without retreating when attention comes. It means trusting that God can hold you even when others see you.

Take this prescription slowly. You are not late. You are learning.

🧬 Spiritual Vitamin: Divine Safety

This spiritual vitamin restores your internal sense of protection. God is not only the One who sees you, He is the One who covers you. Taking this truth daily until visibility no longer feels like danger.

🕊 Holy Spirit Consult

Ask honestly:
- Where did I learn that being seen was unsafe?
- What am I protecting myself from now?
- What would safety look like if God defined it?

Listen without rushing.

🙏 Guided Prayer

"God, I learned to hide because I didn't feel safe. I protected myself by disappearing. Heal the fear that tells me visibility will harm me. Teach me how to be seen without losing myself. Remind me that You are my covering. Amen."

📝 Journal Pages: Relearning Safety

Write gently:

- When did invisibility become protection for me?

____

____

____

- What parts of myself still feel unsafe to show?

____

____

____

- What would it look like to trust God with my visibility?

____

____

____

You did not hide because you were weak. You hid because you were surviving. Now, you are allowed to live.

Chapter 8:

YOU DON'T KNOW HOW TO RECEIVE WHAT YOU'VE ALWAYS GIVEN

SYMPTOM: Emotional Receiving Deficit And The Inability To Accept Care

One of the most overlooked symptoms of invisibility trauma is not exhaustion, fear, or self-doubt, it is the inability to receive. After years of being the one who gives, carries, supports, notices, and holds space for others, receiving begins to feel unfamiliar, uncomfortable, and even threatening. You are skilled at pouring out. You are practicing at showing up. You are fluent in service. But when the direction shifts when someone offers care, affirmation, rest, or attention, you freeze.

This symptom does not mean you are ungrateful. It means your nervous system was trained for output, not intake. Receiving requires vulnerability. It requires presence. It requires letting someone see you without performing, fixing, or helping. And for someone who learned to survive by being useful rather than known, receiving feels destabilizing. You don't know where to put your hands. You don't know what's expected of you. You don't know how to exist without contributing something in return. So, you deflect. You laugh at compliments. You minimize offers of help. You insist you're fine when you're not. You say "you don't have to" when someone tries to care for you. Not because you don't want to care, but because you don't know how to hold it safely.

This symptom often shows up as discomfort when attention is focused on you. When someone asks how *you* are doing, and waits for an answer, you feel exposed. When someone wants to do something *for* you, guilt rises. When someone notices your effort and names it, you feel awkward, even suspicious. You may wonder what they want, what the catch is, or how long it will last.

Receiving feelings conditional because your history taught you that care was rare and inconsistent. You learned that being needed was safer than being cared for. When you give, you control the interaction. When you serve, you remain useful. When you help, you stay necessary. 
But when you receive, you are at risk of disappointment. Care might stop. Attention might fade. Support might come with strings attached. So, your system protects you by keeping you in the role you know best, the giver.

Over time, this pattern becomes identity-shaping. You begin to believe that love is something you earn, not something you are allowed to receive freely. You feel more comfortable offering than accepting. You trust yourself to give, but not others to give to you. You associate receiving with debt, obligation, or vulnerability rather than nourishment.

This is how invisibility trauma distorts love. You may notice that even with God, receiving feels difficult. You serve Him faithfully but struggle to believe He delights in you. You obey but feel uncomfortable resting. You pray, but default to doing rather than being. You are comfortable working *for* God, but uneasy being loved *by* Him without performance.

This symptom can create emotional starvation in plain sight. You may be surrounded by people, serving constantly, involved deeply, and still feel empty. Not because love isn't present, but because you don't know how to let it in. You block nourishment without realizing it. You remain strong while quietly longing to be held, noticed, cared for, and restored. And because receiving feels foreign, you tell yourself you don't need it. But the truth is simpler and harder: you were never taught how.

TEACHING: God Designed You To Be Both A Giver And A Receiver

God never intended giving to replace receiving. In His design, love flows both ways. Output without intake is not holiness, it is depletion. Even in Scripture, God repeatedly emphasizes receiving as an act of humility, not weakness. Receiving requires trust. To receive requires surrender. To receive requires admitting need.

Jesus Himself modeled receiving. He received care from friends. He accepted hospitality. He allowed women to minister to Him. He rested. He withdrew. He did not rush to prove usefulness. He did not refuse to maintain authority. He did not confuse strength with self-sufficiency. He understood that receiving did not diminish His calling, it sustained it.

This teaching challenges the belief that receiving makes you burdensome. You are not a burden for needing care. You are human. The idea that you must always be the strong one is not spiritual, it is unsustainable. God does not call you to one-sided love. He calls you into mutuality.

Receiving does not mean losing control. It means sharing it. Healing begins when you stop viewing care as something you owe back immediately. Love is not a transaction. Rest is not debt. Support is not  something you must repay to deserve. God gives freely, not conditionally. And He invites you to learn how to receive freely, without shame.

You are not meant to earn nourishment. You are meant to be sustained by it. When you allow yourself to receive, slowly, imperfectly, without apology, you begin restoring balance to your emotional and spiritual life. Giving becomes joyful again. Service becomes overflow, not obligation. Love becomes mutual, not one-sided. God does not ask you to stop giving. He asks you to stop starving.

💊 Faith Prescription: Practicing Receiving Without Guilt

This prescription invites you to practice accepting care without explaining, deflecting, or compensating. Start small. Let someone help. Let someone listen. Let someone affirm you. Resist the urge to immediately give something back. Receiving is not selfish. It is necessary.

🧬 Spiritual Vitamin: Grace Without Strings

This spiritual vitamin restores your ability to accept love without conditions. God's grace does not require repayment. Taking this truth daily until receiving no longer feels dangerous.

🕊 Holy Spirit Consult

Ask gently:
- Where do I deflect care automatically?
- What does receiving trigger in me?
- What would it mean to trust love without control?

Listen without rushing to fix.

🙏 Guided Prayer

"God, I confess that I don't know how to receive. I learned to give because it felt safer than being cared for. Heal the fear that tells me receiving is dangerous. Teach me how to accept love without guilt. Restore balance where I've only poured out. Amen."

📝 Journal Pages: Learning To Let Love In

Write honestly:

- What feels hardest for me to receive?

____

____

____

____

____

- Where did I learn that giving was safer than receiving?

____

____

____

____

____

- What would change if I believed I could be loved freely?

____

____

____

____

____

You were never meant to only pour out. You were meant to be filled.

Chapter 9:

YOU DON'T TRUST LOVE THAT DOESN'T NEED YOU

SYMPTOM: Conditional Worth And The Fear Of Being Unnecessary

One of the most destabilizing symptoms of invisibility trauma emerges when love shows up without demand. When someone offers care without asking for anything in return, instead of relief, you feel uneasy. Instead of resting, you feel tension. Instead of gratitude, you feel suspicion. Somewhere deep inside, a quiet alarm goes off: *If they don't need me, will they still want me?*

This symptom is not about arrogance or control. It is about survival. You learned to secure connection through usefulness. Being helpful, available, reliable, and needed became your way of staying connected. Love, in your experience, was often reinforced by function. You were valued when you carried something. You were noticed when you contributed something. You were kept close when you made yourself indispensable. So, when love arrives without expectation, it doesn't feel safe. It feels unfamiliar.

This symptom often shows up as discomfort in relationships where you are not required to perform. You may feel restless when someone doesn't ask much of you. You may feel unsure of your place when you are not actively contributing. You may feel anxious when a relationship feels stable without your effort. And without realizing it, you may begin *creating* usefulness just to feel secure again.

You offer help that wasn't requested. You insert yourself where you aren't needed. You overextend to justify your presence. Not because you want control, but because stillness feels like disappearance. This symptom teaches you to equate being needed with being loved. And when that equation goes unchallenged, it begins shaping how you choose relationships. You gravitate toward people, roles, and environments where your usefulness is obvious. You feel most comfortable where there is a problem to solve, a role to fill, or a gap to cover. Calm, reciprocal relationships feel boring or suspicious. You wonder what your purpose is there.

The danger is that this pattern keeps you emotionally busy but spiritually starved. Love that does not require you feels unsafe because it threatens the identity you built around usefulness. If you are not needed, who are you? If you are not fixing, serving, carrying, or rescuing, what value do you bring? These questions are terrifying when your sense of worth was forged in survival.

This symptom also affects how you relate to God. You may be deeply committed to serving Him, but uncomfortable resting with Him. You may feel closest to God when you are doing something for Him, but distant when you are simply being with Him. You may struggle to believe He delights in you apart from obedience. You trust God as a Master but hesitate to trust Him as a Father who loves you without conditions. This is not lack of faith. This is distorted attachment.

Over time, conditional worth leads to quiet anxiety. You feel pressure to stay useful. You feel uneasy when you slow down. You fear becoming irrelevant. And because you don't want to lose connection, you keep giving, keep doing, keep offering, often at the expense of rest, joy, and authenticity.

The hardest part of this symptom is that it masquerades as devotion. You look committed. You look faithful. You look generous. But underneath, you are exhausted by the unspoken fear that love might disappear if you stop performing.

TEACHING: God's Love Is Not Sustained By Your Usefulness

God does not love you because He needs you. He loves you because He chose you. That distinction is critical for healing. When love is rooted in need, it is fragile. When love is rooted in choice, it is secure.

God was complete before you ever existed. Your obedience does not fill a gap in Him. Your service does not sustain Him. Your usefulness does not increase His affection. He invites you into partnership not because He lacks something, but because He desires relationship.

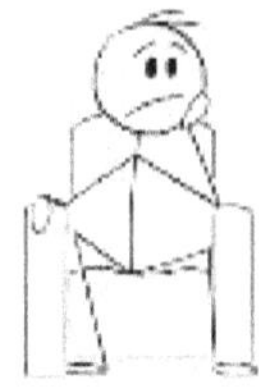

This teaching challenges the belief that usefulness equals worth. In Scripture, God repeatedly affirms identity before assignment. He calls people beloved before He calls them useful. He establishes worth before He gives responsibility. And when people confuse their role with their value, God consistently interrupts that pattern, often through rest, waiting, or seasons of stillness.

Love that does not require you is not meaningless. It is secure. Healing begins when you allow yourself to believe that being chosen is different from being needed. God does not need you to earn your place with Him. He already gave it to you. Service flows from belonging, not the other way around.

When you stop trying to secure love through usefulness, relationships begin to change. You no longer panic when you are not needed. You no longer overextend to stay relevant. You begin trusting that your presence alone is enough.

God does not withdraw when you rest. He does not lose interest when you pause. He does not forget you when you are still. His love is not maintained by your effort. It is sustained by His nature.

💊 Faith Prescription: Belonging Without Performance

This prescription invites you to practice being present without proving value. It asks you to notice when you are trying to earn connection and gently stop. Belonging without performance feels uncomfortable at first, but it is the path to true rest.

Take this prescription daily by reminding yourself: *I am loved because I am chosen, not because I am needed.*

🧬 Spiritual Vitamin: Secure Attachment In God

This spiritual vitamin restores trust in love that does not demand output. God's attachment to you is secure. Take this truth daily until usefulness no longer feels like survival.

🕊 Holy Spirit Consult

Ask honestly:
- Where do I feel anxious when I am not needed?
- What does stillness trigger in me?
- How have I tied my worth to usefulness?

Listen without defending.

🙏 Guided Prayer

"God, I confess that I equated being needed with being loved. I feared that if I stopped performing, I would disappear. Heal the places where usefulness replaced belonging. Teach me how to rest in love that doesn't require me. Remember that I am chosen, not earned. Amen."

📝 Journal Pages: Untangling Worth From Usefulness

Write honestly:
- Where do I feel most valuable, and why?

- What scares me about not being needed?

- What would change if I trusted love without conditions?

You were never loved because you were useful. You were useful because you loved.

Chapter 10:

YOU MISTOOK ENDURANCE FOR HEALING

SYMPTOM: Functional Survival And The Illusion Of Strength

One of the most deceptive symptoms of invisibility trauma is the belief that because you endured, you healed. You look back at everything you survived: the neglect, the silence, the waiting, the being overlooked, and you tell yourself that you must be fine now. After all, you didn't fall apart. You didn't quit. You didn't collapse publicly. You kept going. You adapted. You learned how to function without acknowledgment, without affirmation, without care. And because you functioned, you assumed you healed. But endurance is not healing. It is survival with stamina.

This symptom forms when pain goes unprocessed for too long. When no one names what happened, when no one apologizes, when no one acknowledges the cost, you move on because you must. Life doesn't pause long enough for you to process what hurts you. Responsibilities continue. Expectations remain. People keep needing you. And because you are capable, you keep meeting the demand.

Over time, functionality becomes your proof of wholeness. You tell yourself that if something were truly wrong, you wouldn't be able to keep showing up. You minimize your pain because it didn't stop you. You dismiss emotional numbness because it doesn't look like breakdown. You ignore exhaustion because you're still productive. You confuse coping with healing, stability with restoration, and endurance with freedom.

This is how invisible wounds stay invisible.

Functional survival teaches you to compartmentalize. You separate what hurts from what works. You put pain in one box and productivity in another. You learn how to operate efficiently without addressing what's unresolved. And because you are good at it, no one questions it. They see strength. They see resilience. They see faithfulness. They don't see the cost.

Eventually, you may notice subtle signs that something is off. You feel disconnected from your emotions. Joy feels distant. Passion feels muted. Hope feels theoretical. You don't feel broken, but you don't feel alive either. You exist in a neutral state, capable, consistent, but flat. This emotional flatlining becomes your new normal, and you mistake it for peace.

But peace does not numb you. Peace integrates with you. This symptom often shows up in spiritual language. You say things like, "I'm over it," "God healed me," or "That was a long time ago," not because it's fully true, but because revisiting it feels unnecessary or risky. You don't want to reopen wounds. You don't want to sound ungrateful. You don't want to feel weak. So, you declare healing prematurely and move on.

But unresolved pain doesn't disappear. It waits. It waits until you slow down. It waits until you stop performing. It waits until you are no longer distracted by survival. Then it resurfaces, not as crisis, but as quiet emptiness. As lack of joy. As fatigue you can't explain. As spiritual dryness. As relational distance. You didn't regress. You didn't fail. You simply reached the end of what endurance can do. Surviving invisibility requires strength. Healing from it requires honesty.

TEACHING: God Heals What You're Willing To Acknowledge

God never confuses endurance with wholeness. He honors your survival, but He does not call it healing. Healing, in God's economy, is not about how well you function, it is about how fully you live. It is not measured by productivity, but by integration. By the reunion of what you survived with who you are becoming.

Throughout Scripture, God consistently invites people to bring what they endured into the light, not to shame them, but to restore them. Jesus never praised people for pretending they were fine. He asked questions. He named himself Wounds. He invited honestly. He healed what was exposed, not what was hidden behind performance. This teaching reframes healing as process, not declaration. You do not heal by announcing that you're healed. You heal by allowing God to touch the places you learned to ignore. You heal by naming the cost of survival. You heal by acknowledging that just because you made it through doesn't mean you came out whole.

God is not offended by your unfinished healing. He is patient with it. Healing requires more than endurance. It requires presence. It requires slowing down long enough to feel what you avoided. It requires trusting that acknowledging pain will not undo you. And it requires releasing the belief that strength means silence. God does not ask you to relive trauma. He asks you to stop denying its impact. When you stop mistaking endurance for healing, something shifts. You give yourself permission to need restoration. You stop rushing closure. You stop minimizing your story. You allow God to meet you where you are, not where you say you should be.

Healing is not the absence of pain. It is the presence of truth. God does not rush this work. He does not demand immediate wholeness. He does not shame you for still needing care. He walks with you through it, patiently, gently, without pressure to perform. You are not behind. You are becoming honest. And honesty is where healing begins.

Faith Prescription: Integration Over Performance

This prescription invites you to stop measuring healing by functionality. Integration means allowing your past, pain, resilience, and hope to exist together without denial. It means giving God access to the parts of you that learned to survive instead of healing. Take this prescription daily by asking: *What am I functioning through that I haven't healed from yet?*

🧬 Spiritual Vitamin: Grace For The Unfinished Places

This spiritual vitamin restores compassion toward yourself. God is not disappointed by your unfinished healing. Take this truth daily until you no longer feel pressured to be "over it."

🕊 Holy Spirit Consult

Ask honestly:

- Where have I confused endurance with healing?
- What pain did I survive but never process?
- What would it mean to heal instead of just cope?

Listen without rushing to resolve.

🙏 Guided Prayer

"God, I confess that I survived things I never healed from. I called endurance peace and coping strength. Heal the places I learned to ignore. Give me courage to slow down and be honest. Restore what survival preserved but healing must transform. Amen."

📝 Journal Pages: Beyond Survival

Write gently and truthfully:

- What did I survive that still affect me?

____

____

____

____

- Where am I functional but not free?

____

____

____

____

- What would healing look like beyond endurance?

____

____

____

____

____

____

You did not fail because you survived. But you don't have to stay in survival forever.

PART III: THE TREATMENT PLAN

PERSONAL NOTES

94

Chapter 11:

YOU'RE AFRAID TO WANT MORE BECAUSE YOU'VE LEARNED TO EXPECT LESS

SYMPTOM: Restricted Desire And The Fear Of Hope

One of the quietest but most limiting symptoms of invisibility trauma is not despair, it is restrained desire. You still want things, but you don't let yourself admit it. You still hope, but only privately, cautiously, with conditions attached. You learned how to survive disappointment by lowering expectations, and over time, that strategy became a way of life. Wanting more began to feel dangerous, because wanting more meant risking the pain of not receiving it.

This symptom doesn't announce itself as hopelessness. It often disguises itself as contentment. You say things like, "I'm fine with whatever," or "I don't need much," or "I've learned not to expect anything." These statements sound mature. They sound spiritual. They sound like acceptance. But beneath them is often grief, grief over desires that were never met, hopes that went unanswered, and dreams that felt foolish to keep alive.

Restricted desire forms as a protective response. When you hoped deeply and were repeatedly overlooked, passed over, or ignored, your system learned that longing leads to pain. So, you adapted. You learned how to want less. You learned how to keep expectations low. You learned how to convince yourself that what you secretly desired wasn't that important anyway. Not because it wasn't meaningful, but because disappointment hurt too much to revisit.

Over time, you may notice that you hesitate when asked what you want. You struggle to articulate dreams. You feel uncomfortable imagining a future that looks different from your present. You may even feel guilty for wanting more, as if desire itself is evidence of ingratitude or lack of faith. You tell yourself that wanting less keeps you humble, that expecting nothing keeps you safe.

But safety purchased at the cost of desire slowly drains life of color. This symptom often shows up as emotional flatness around hope. You don't feel excited about the future. You don't feel devastated either. You exist in the middle, stable, steady, but uninspired. You avoid dreaming big because dreaming big reminds you of times you hoped and were disappointed. You choose realism over longing.

You choose practicality over possibility. And you call it wisdom. Yet underneath that "wisdom" is fear. Fear of hoping again. Fear of being let down again. Fear of wanting something God might not give. Invisibility trauma teaches you that desire is risky because it exposes vulnerability. When no one noticed you're longing before, you learned to silence it. You stopped sharing your hopes. You stopped praying boldly. You stopped imagining outcomes that would require God to show up visibly. You learned how to settle, not because you lacked faith, but because you were tired of being disappointed.

This is how desire becomes self-censored.

You don't stop believing God can do more. You stop believing He will do it *for you.* You may still celebrate other people's breakthroughs but quietly assume yours won't come. You tell yourself that being unseen means learning to live without expectation. And slowly, hope becomes theoretical instead of personal.

TEACHING: God Is Not Threatened By Your Desire For More

God never asked you to stop wanting. Desire is not the enemy of faith; it is often the evidence of it. Desire reflects trust that something good is possible. It reflects belief that life can be fuller, deeper, more alive. When desire goes dormant, it is not because faith matured; it is often because disappointment accumulated.

Scripture consistently affirms desire as something God honors, not punishes. God invites people to ask, seek, knock, not cautiously, but boldly. He does not shame longing. He responds to it. And while He does not fulfill every desire in the way we expect, He never asks us to stop desiring altogether.

This teaching reframes desire as courage rather than entitlement. You are not greedy for wanting more. You are not ungrateful for hoping again. You are not immature for dreaming beyond what you've experienced. God is not offended by your longing; He is often the One who planted it. Desire becomes dangerous only when it replaces trust, but suppressed desire becomes dangerous when it replaces honesty.

God does not heal disappointment by numbing desire. He heals it by restoring hope. When you stop allowing yourself to want more, you limit not only your joy, but your willingness to partner with God in the future He is shaping. Desire keeps you open. It keeps you engaged. It keeps you moving forward. Without it, life becomes maintenance instead of expectancy.

 God is not asking you to demand outcomes. He is inviting you to risk hope again. Healing begins when you allow yourself to want without guarantees. When you let yourself dream without controlling the result. When you stop punishing yourself for past disappointment by restricting future possibilities.

Desire does not make you weak. It makes you alive. And God specializes in restoring what went dormant.

🔖 Faith Prescription: Hope Without Guarantees

This prescription invites you to practice wanting again without attaching certainty to outcome. Hope without guarantees means you allow yourself to desire even when you cannot predict the result. It means trusting God with the outcome instead of silencing the longing.

Take this prescription daily by asking: *What have I stopped wanting because it felt safer not to hope?*

🧬 Spiritual Vitamin: Courage to Desire Again

This spiritual vitamin restores bravery in longing. God is not punishing you for wanting more. Take this truth daily until desire no longer feels dangerous.

🕊 Holy Spirit Consult

Ask honestly:

- Where have I learned to expect less to avoid disappointment?
- What desires have I silenced to stay safe?
- What would it look like to hope again without control?

Listen without censoring the response

🙏 Guided Prayer

"God, I confess that disappointment taught me to want less. I learned to silence desire to avoid pain. Heal the fear that tells me hope is dangerous.

Restore my courage to want again. Teach me how to desire without demanding. Amen."

📝 Journal Pages: Reawakening Desire

Write gently and honestly:

- What do I want but hesitate to admit?

____

____

____

____

- When did wanting to begin to feel unsafe?

____

____

____

____

- What would change if I allowed myself to hope again?

____

____

____

____

You were not wrong for hoping. You were wounded by disappointment. And now, you are allowed to want again.

Chapter 12:

YOU CONFUSED PEACE WITH EMOTIONAL NUMBNESS

SYMPTOM: Emotional Numbing Mistaken for Spiritual Peace

One of the most misleading symptoms of invisibility trauma is emotional numbing that gets labeled as peace. You are no longer as reactive. You are no longer disappointed. You are no  longer as affected by being overlooked. And on the surface, this feels like progress. You tell yourself you've matured. You say you've healed. You believe you've found peace. But underneath that calm exterior, something essential has gone quiet, not just pain, but joy, passion, excitement, and emotional color.

This symptom develops when feeling becomes too costly. After years of being unseen, hoping without response, desiring without fulfillment, and giving without reciprocation, your system learns that feeling deeply leads to disappointment. So, it adapts by lowering emotional intensity across the board. You don't just stop feeling hurt, you stop feeling much of anything. You exist in a steady, controlled state where nothing touches too deeply. This feels safe. Predictable. Manageable. And because you are no longer visibly distressed, people may even affirm this change. They say you seem calm. Grounded. At peace. Spiritually mature. And you accept those labels because they align with what you want to believe. But emotional numbing is not peace. It is protection.

Peace integrates emotion. Numbness suppresses it. This symptom often shows up as a lack of reaction rather than a lack of pain. You still notice when you're overlooked, but it doesn't sting as sharply. You still experience disappointment, but it doesn't move you. You stop celebrating wins fully. You stop grieving losses deeply. You stop feeling anticipation. Life becomes emotionally flat, neither overwhelming nor fulfilling. At first, this flatness feels like relief.

You are no longer riding emotional highs and lows. You are no longer destabilized by what others do or don't do. You feel in control. But over time, you begin to realize that control came at a cost. You don't feel alive the way you used to. You don't feel connected to joy. You don't feel stirred by hope. You feel steady, but empty.

This symptom often disguises itself as spiritual detachment. You still believe in God. You still show up. You still pray. But your relationship with Him feels muted. Worship feels more intellectual than emotional. Prayer feels routine rather than relational. You trust God, but you don't feel close to Him. And because you've learned to function without emotional connection, you assume this is normal.

But it's not whole.

It's survival with emotional volume turned down.

Emotional numbing could feel preferable to pain, especially if pain went unacknowledged for too long. When no one noticed your hurt before, you learned not to express it. When longing went unmet, you learned not to feel it. When hope led to disappointment, you learned to shut it down. Numbing was never a choice; it was a response. And now, it has become your baseline.

TEACHING: God's Peace Does Not Require You To Go Emotionally Silent

Biblical peace is not the absence of emotion. It is the presence of wholeness. It is not numbness, it is integration. God's peace does not dull your feelings; it stabilizes them. It does not silence your heart; it secures it.

Throughout Scripture, people who walked closely with God still felt deeply. They grieved. They rejoiced. They lamented. They celebrated. Emotional expression was not a sign of weak faith; it was evidence of honesty. God never asked His people to stop feeling. He invited them to bring their feelings to Him.

This teaching reframes peace as *capacity*, not shutdown. True peace expands your ability to feel without being overwhelmed. It allows you to experience joy without fear and sorrow without collapse. Emotional numbing, on the other hand, reduces capacity. It limits range. It keeps you safe from pain but also distant from delight.

God is not asking you to return to emotional chaos. He is inviting you out of emotional silence. Healing begins when you allow yourself to feel again, slowly, gently, without judgment. It means allowing joy to return without bracing for loss. It means letting sadness surface without shaming it. It means trusting that emotions are not threats to faith, but companions on the journey of restoration. God's peace is not fragile. It does not require emotional suppression to survive. When you stop confusing numbness with peace, you give God access to restore emotional life. You stop settling for neutrality. You begin opening yourself to wholeness. You learn that calm does not require disconnection, and that safety does not require silence. Peace does not make you less human. It makes you more whole.

💊 Faith Prescription: Feeling Without Fear

This prescription invites you to gently re-engage with your emotional life. Feeling without fear means allowing emotions to surface without rushing to control or suppress them. It means trusting that God can hold what you feel. Take this prescription daily by noticing what you feel without correcting it.

🍬 Spiritual Vitamin: Emotional Wholeness

This spiritual vitamin restores permission to feel fully. God does not heal by numbing, He heals by integrating. Take this truth daily until feeling no longer feels dangerous.

🕊 Holy Spirit Consult

Ask honestly:

- Where have I shut down emotionally to stay safe?
- What emotions feel most uncomfortable for me now?
- What would it look like to feel again without fear?

Listen gently, without rushing to resolve.

🙏 Guided Prayer

God, I confess that I confused numbness with peace. I silenced my emotions to survive disappointment. Heal the places where I shut down to stay safe. Restore my ability to feel without fear. Teach me the peace that holds emotion, not erases it. Amen.

📝 Journal Pages: From Numbness To Wholeness

Write honestly and slowly:

- What emotions have I shut down?

____

____

____

____

- When did feeling become unsafe for me?

- What would peace look like if I were fully alive?

You were not weak for numbing. You were protecting yourself. Now, you are allowed to feel again.

PERSONAL NOTES

Chapter 13:

YOU LEARNED TO CALL LONELINESS "INDEPENDENCE"

SYMPTOM: Hyper-Independence Masked As Strength

One of the most socially rewarded symptoms of invisibility trauma is hyper-independence. You learned how to do everything yourself. You don't ask for help. You don't lean. Don't wait. You figure it out, handle it, fix it, and move on. And because this looks competent, capable, and mature, no one questions it. In fact, people often admire it. They call you strong. Resilient. Self-sufficient. What they don't see is loneliness underneath independence.

This symptom develops when dependence felt dangerous or disappointing. When you reached out and no one responded. When you asked and were ignored. When you needed support and learned it wasn't coming. Each unanswered need taught your system a lesson: *needing people hurts*. So, you adapted. You stopped expecting help. You stopped requesting care. You stopped believing anyone would show up consistently. And independence became your protection.

First, hyper-independence feels empowering. You don't have to wait for anyone. You don't have to explain yourself. You don't risk disappointment. You stay in control. You rely on yourself and keep moving. But over time, that control turns into isolation. You stop sharing burdens because you don't believe anyone will carry them well. You stop inviting people into your inner world because it feels intrusive. You build a life where you are competent, but alone.

This symptom often shows up as discomfort with reliance. You feel uneasy when someone offers help. You feel guilty when you need support. You feel weak for wanting connection. You pride yourself on not needing much. You tell yourself you prefer independence. And sometimes you do. But often, independence became preference only after dependence became painful.

Hyper-independence convinces you that closeness is optional. You maintain relationships, but at a distance. You engage, but selectively. You allow people into your life, but not into your vulnerability. You share updates, not struggles. You offer support but rarely ask for it. And while this keeps you safe from disappointment, it also keeps you disconnected from intimacy.

Loneliness creeps in quietly here. You may be surrounded by people and still feel alone. You may be admired and still feel unseen. You may be capable and still feel unsupported. Because independence cannot replace connections. It can only postpone the ache of its absence.

This symptom also affects how you relate to God. You trust Him, but you keep emotional distance. You believe, but you self-manage. You pray, but you don't lean. You ask for guidance, but you carry the weight alone. You don't expect God to show up relationally, you expect yourself to handle it spiritually. Hyper-independence does not mean you don't want connection. It means you don't trust it. And over time, that mistrust becomes identity. You stop seeing yourself as someone who can be supported. You see yourself as the supporter. The carrier. The one who doesn't need much. And in doing so, you quietly accept loneliness as the price of safety.

TEACHING: God Did Not Design You To Heal Alone

God never designed independence to replace connection. From the beginning, His declaration was clear: *it is not good for humans to be alone*. Not weak humans. Not broken humans. Humans. Need was never a flaw in God's design; it was part of it.

This teaching reframes independence through the lens of interdependence. God does not ask you to become helpless.

He invites you into shared strength. Into community where burdens are distributed, not hoarded. Into relationships where support flows both ways.

Jesus Himself modeled dependence. He asked for help. He accepted care. He allowed others to walk with Him. He did not carry everything alone. Strength in Scripture is never portrayed as isolation. It is portrayed as connection rooted in trust. Hyper-independence is not holiness; it is a response to unmet need.

 God does not heal by teaching you to need nothing. He heals by restoring safe connections. Healing begins when you allow yourself to acknowledge that independence was a coping strategy, not a calling. That doing life alone kept you safe, but it also kept you lonely. God is not asking you to abandon self-reliance entirely. He is asking you to loosen its grip so connection can be returned.

You do not lose strength by letting someone help you. You do not lose dignity by needing support. You do not lose faith by learning. God's design for healing includes people, not as replacements for Him, but as reflections of His care. Community is not a threat to safety when it is rooted in truth, boundaries, and mutuality. You were never meant to be the only one carrying your life.

💊 Faith Prescription: Practicing Interdependence

This prescription invites you to slowly reintroduce shared strength into your life. Practicing interdependence does not mean oversharing or abandoning boundaries. It means allowing safe people to participate in your healing. Take this prescription gently by letting one person support you in one small way.

🧬 Spiritual Vitamin: Belonging Without Control

This spiritual vitamin restores trust in connection without requiring self-management. God does not ask you to control every outcome. Take this truth daily until belonging no longer feels risky.

🕊 Holy Spirit Consult

Ask honestly:
- Where did I learn that needing others is unsafe?
- What does independence protect me from?
- Who might be safe to let closer?

Listen without forcing answers.

🙏 Guided Prayer

"God, I confess that I learned to do life alone. I called independence strength because dependence hurt. Healing the fear that tells me connection is dangerous. Teach me how to learn without losing myself. Restore belonging to where loneliness took root. Amen."

📝 Journal Pages: From Isolation To Connection

Write gently:
- Where am I overly independent?

____

____

____

____

- What am I afraid would happen if I asked for help?

- What would safe connection look like for me now?

You were not strong because you did it alone. You did it alone because you were surviving. Now, you are allowed to belong.

PERSONAL NOTES

Chapter 14:

YOU STOPPED LETTING YOURSELF BE KNOWN

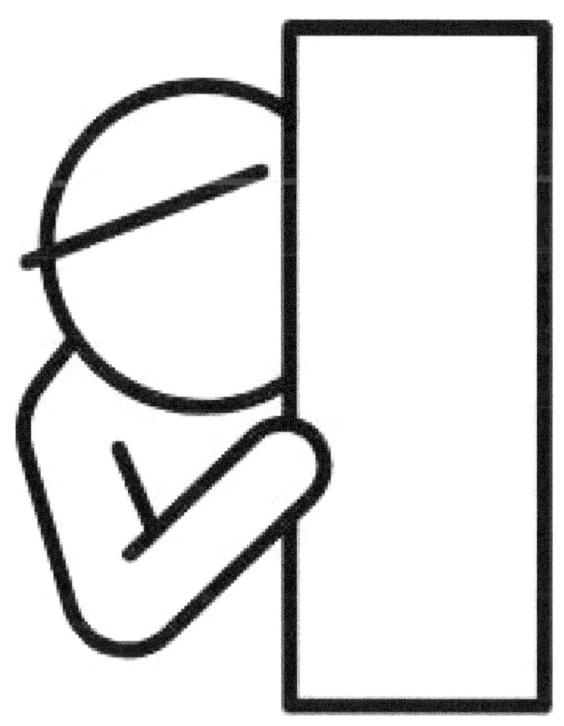

SYMPTOM: Selective Disclosure And The Habit Of Staying Surface-Level

 One of the most painful outcomes of invisibility trauma is not that you lack relationships, but that you no longer allow yourself to be *known* within them. You may have people around you. You may be connected, involved, even admired. And yet, very few, if any, truly know you. Not because they never asked, but because somewhere along the way, you learned that being fully known was risky.

This symptom develops when visibility is not safe or rewarded. When you opened and were misunderstood. When vulnerability was met with silence, dismissal, advice instead of empathy, or exposure instead of protection. Each of those moments taught your system a lesson: *sharing costs more than it gives.* So, you adapted by becoming selective. Not dishonest, just edited.

Selective disclosure does not mean you lie. It means you curate. You share facts without feelings. Updates without depth. Stories without impact. You talk about what happened, but not how it affected you. You let people see your competence, your humor, your faith, but not your confusion, grief, anger, or longing. You become excellent at conversation while remaining emotionally unavailable.

This symptom often masquerades as privacy. You tell yourself you are just reserved. You say you prefer to keep things to yourself. You believe not everyone deserves access to your inner world, and that may be true. But invisibility trauma takes that wisdom and turns it into isolation. You stop letting *anyone* see beyond the surface, even those who have earned trust.

Over time, selective disclosure becomes default. You don't consciously decide what to withhold; you instinctively avoid depth.

When conversations turn personal, you redirect. When someone asks a question that touches something tender, you minimize. When opportunities for intimacy arise, you keep them light. You do this not to deceive, but to protect.

Protection, however, slowly becomes disconnected. You may notice that relationships feel unsatisfying. People know *about* you, but not *you*. You feel unseen even when surrounded. You feel lonely in the presence of others. And because you are the one withholding, you blame yourself quietly for the distance, without recognizing that withholding was something you learned to survive.

This symptom also affects your relationship with God. You pray, but selectively. You bring requests, but not confusion. You offer praise, but not disappointment. You confess behavior, but not grief. You talk to God about what you think you should feel, not what you feel. Over time, intimacy with Him becomes transactional instead of relational.

When you stop letting yourself be known, connection becomes impossible, not because love isn't present, but because access is restricted. And the most painful part is this: you crave being known deeply, but you no longer trust it enough to allow it.

TEACHING: God Heals Through Honest Exposure, Not Performance

God has never healed people through concealment. He heals through truths, revealed, and held safely in His presence. From the beginning, God invites honesty, not polish. He does not ask you to impress Him with your strength or faith. He asks you to bring your whole self, unedited.

Throughout Scripture, God consistently meets people in moments of exposure. When they tell the truth. When they admit fear. When they voice confusion. When they name grief. Being known by God is not about information, it is about intimacy. And intimacy cannot exist without vulnerability.

 This teaching reframes being known as healing rather than danger. You were not created to be fully self-contained. You were designed for mutual knowing, first with God, then with others. Being known does not mean being unprotected. It means being seen in places where you are honored, not exploited. God does not invite you to reckless vulnerability. He invites you to *be safe honesty*.

Healing begins when you allow yourself to be known again, slowly, wisely, intentionally. Not by everyone. Not all at once. But by God, first and fully. When you stop editing your prayers. When you stop filtering your emotions. When you stop pretending you are okay when you are not.

God already knows you. He is waiting for you to agree with Him. When you allow God access to the parts you learned to hide, restoration begins. You stop performing spirituality and start experiencing relationships. And from that foundation, you can begin discerning who else may be safe to let closer. You do not have to choose between safety and privacy. With God, you can have both.

💊 Faith Prescription: Practicing Honest Presence

This prescription invites you to show up honestly, without polishing, minimizing, or spiritualizing your reality. Honest presence means telling the truth about where you are, even when it feels uncomfortable.

Take this prescription daily by naming one real emotion in prayer without correcting it.

🧬 Spiritual Vitamin: Truth Without Consequences

This spiritual vitamin restores trust that honesty will not lead to punishment or rejection. God does not withdraw when you tell the truth. Take this truth daily until honesty feels safer than silence.

🕊 Holy Spirit Consult

Ask gently:

- What parts of me do I hide automatically?
- Where did I learn that being known was unsafe?
- What would it look like to be honest without fear?

Listen without rushing to fix.

🙏 Guided Prayer

God, I confess that I learned to hide to stay safe. I filtered myself to avoid being hurt. Healing the fear that tells me honesty is dangerous. Teach me how to be known without losing myself. Restore intimacy where protection became distance. Amen.

📝 Journal Pages: Letting Yourself Be Known Again

Write slowly and truthfully:

- What do people know *about* me, but not *about* me?

____

____

- What am I afraid it would happen if I were fully known?

- What would honest connection look like now?

You were not wrong for protecting yourself. But you do not have to stay hidden forever. You are allowed to be known.

PERSONAL NOTES

PART IV: AFTERCARE

PERSONAL NOTES

Chapter 15:

YOU LEARNED TO STOP ASKING FOR WHAT YOU NEED

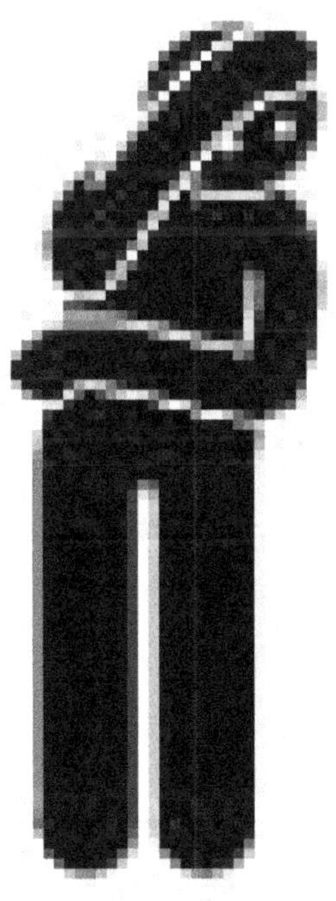

SYMPTOM: Need Suppression And The Habit Of Self-Silencing

One of the most deeply ingrained symptoms of invisibility trauma is not the absence of need, but the suppression of it. You still have need emotional, relational, spiritual, but you no longer name them. You no longer ask them to be met. You no longer believe they are worth the risk of disappointment. Somewhere along the way, asking stopped feeling safe, so you stopped doing it.

This symptom often forms in environments where needs were ignored, minimized, or treated as inconvenient. You asked once and were overlooked. You asked again and were misunderstood. You asked a third time and were made to feel dramatic, demanding, or ungrateful. Each experience taught your nervous system the same lesson: *asking leads to pain*. So, you adapted by going quiet. 

Need suppression does not look like indifference. It looks like self-sufficiency. It looks like phrases such as, "I'm fine," "I don't need anything," or "It's not a big deal." You become skilled at meeting your own needs internally or doing without. You stop reaching out. You stop expressing longing. You convince yourself that needing less is strength.

But needing less is not the same as being whole.

Over time, suppressed needs don't disappear, they turn inward. You feel unexplained sadness. You feel chronic fatigue. You feel distant from others even when you'represent. You may feel frustrated or resentful without knowing why. These are not signs of weakness; they are signals that something essential has been silenced.

This symptom often pairs with guilt. You feel guilty for wanting support. Guilty for needing reassurance. Guilty for asking for time, care, attention, or rest. You tell yourself other people have bigger problems. You tell yourself you should be grateful. You tell yourself God understands, even when no one else does. And slowly, your voice disappears from your own story.

Need suppression also affects your relationship with God. You pray responsibly instead of honestly. You thank Him for what you have but hesitate to ask for what you long for. You assume He already knows your needs, so you don't say them out loud. Over time, prayer becomes cautious. Controlled. Safe. But God never asked you to be silent about your need.

The most painful part of this symptom is that it convinces you that asking is a failure. That expressing need makes you weak. That voicing desire makes you vulnerable in ways you cannot afford. And so, you survive quietly, capable, composed, and alone.

TEACHING: God Does Not Heal Needs You Never Name

God has never shamed need. From Genesis to the Gospels, God consistently invites people to ask. To cry out. To knock. To request daily bread. Need is not evidence of spiritual immaturity; it is evidence of humanity. Suppressing need does not make you stronger, it makes you isolated.

This teaching reframes asking as an act of trust, not desperation. God already knows your needs, but He invites you to name them because naming creates relationship. When you ask, you acknowledge dependence, not helplessness, but connection. God does not respond to silence with approval. He responds to honesty with care.

Jesus repeatedly asked people what they wanted, even when the answer seemed obvious. Not because He lacked awareness, but because healing requires voice. What your name can be addressed. What you suppress remains hidden. Healing begins when you give yourself permission to ask again. Not demanding. Not insist. Ask.

Asking does not guarantee immediate fulfillment, but it restores dignity. It reconnects you to your own humanity. It reminds you that your needs matter enough to be spoken aloud. God does not punish you for asking. He meets you in it.

You are not weak for needing support. You are not selfish for wanting care. You are not faithless for asking God to show up. God is not threatened by your needs. He is moved by them. When you stop silencing yourself, something shifts. You begin reinhabiting your voice. You begin trusting that your inner world matters. You begin by allowing connection to form again not perfectly, not instantly, but honestly. God does not ask you to go without. He asks you to come to Him.

💊 Faith Prescription: Asking Without Apology

This prescription invites you to practice naming your needs without explaining or justifying them. Asking without apology means releasing the belief that need makes you burdensome. Take this prescription daily by naming one need, to God or to a safe person, without minimizing it.

🧬 Spiritual Vitamin: Permission To Need

This spiritual vitamin restores your right to have needs. God does not love you less when you ask. Take this truth daily until need no longer feels like failure.

🕊 Holy Spirit Consult

Ask gently:

- What needs have I stopped naming?
- Where did I learn that asking was unsafe?
- What would it look like to trust God with my need again?

Listen without rushing to resolve.

🙏 Guided Prayer

"God, I confess that I stopped asking because it hurt to be ignored. I silenced my needs to survive disappointment. Heal the places where I learned to go without voice. Teach me how to ask without fear or shame. Restore trust where silence took over. Amen."

📝 Journal Pages: Reclaiming Your Voice

Write honestly:

- What do I need but hesitate to say out loud?

____

____

____

____

- When did you begin to feel unsafe?

____

____

____

____

- What would change if I believed my needs mattered?

____

____

____

____

You were not wrong for going quiet. You were protecting yourself. Now, you are allowed to speak again.

PERSONAL NOTES

____

____

____

____

____

____

____

____

____

____

Chapter 16:

YOU APOLOGIZE FOR EXISTING

SYMPTOM: Chronic Self-Minimization And Reflexive Apologizing

One of the most telling symptoms of invisibility trauma is not loud  insecurity; it is quiet, constant apologizing. You apologize for speaking. You apologize for needing time. You apologize for emotions. You apologize for asking questions. You apologize for taking up space, for having opinions, for existing in ways that might inconvenience someone else. The apologies come out before you even think about them. They are reflexive, automatic, and deeply ingrained.

This symptom forms in environments where your presence felt tolerated rather than welcomed. Where attention felt scarce. Where expressing yourself seemed to disrupt the flow or draw unwanted scrutiny. Over time, you learned that things are shrinking smoothly over. Apologizing became a way to preempt rejection. If you apologized first, maybe no one would be annoyed. If you minimized yourself early, maybe you wouldn't be dismissed later.

So, you learned to say "sorry" when nothing was wrong. You apologize when you take too long. You apologize when you ask for clarity. You apologize when you express emotion. You apologize when you exist with needs, limits, or preferences. Not because you believe you've done something wrong, but because you learned that your presence requires permission. This symptom often hides behind politeness. You tell yourself you're just being courteous. Considerate. Respectful. And while kindness is not the problem, chronic self-minimization is. Over-apologizing trains your mind to associate existence with offense. You begin believing that you are always one step away from being too slow, too needy, too visible. And so, you cushion yourself with apology, hoping it will soften the impact of being seen.

Over time, this pattern reshapes identity. You begin second-guessing yourself constantly. You hesitate before speaking. You mentally rehearse interactions, scanning for ways you might inconvenience someone. You feel guilty for asserting boundaries. You feel uncomfortable receiving attention without deflecting it. And when something genuinely goes wrong, the apology carries more shame than responsibility. This is not humility. It is conditioned fear.

This symptom also bleeds into your relationship with God. You approach Him cautiously. You apologize for your prayers. You say things like, "I know others have bigger problems," or "Sorry to bother You." You pray as if you are interrupting rather than approaching a Father. You believe God loves you, but you act as though His time is limited and your presence is costly.

Apologizing for existence is not reverence. It is learned unworthiness. And the most painful part is this: you don't even realize how much space you've surrendered. You've made yourself small so long that it feels normal. You've apologized invisibility.

TEACHING: God Never Asked You To Apologize For Taking Up Space

God does not create people as interruptions. He creates them as intention. Your existence is not an inconvenience that needs softening. It is a deliberate act of design. When God formed you, He did not hesitate. He did not apologize. He did not create you reluctantly.

This teaching reframes presence as permission, not intrusion. Throughout Scripture, God consistently affirms people before they ever do anything useful. He calls them chosen, beloved, seen. He invites them to speak, to ask, to come boldly. There is no apology required to approach Him. No minimizing necessary to be heard. God does not respond well to self-erasure He responds to truth.

Jesus never apologized for taking up space. He asked questions. He spoke openly. He rested publicly. He withdrew when needed. He asserted boundaries without guilt. His humility did not erase His presence. It anchored it. God is not asking you to become demanding or entitled. He is asking you to stop treating your existence as a problem. You do not need to shrink to be accepted. You do not need to apologize for deserving care. You do not need to earn the right to be present.

Healing begins when you notice the apology and pause. Instead of saying "sorry for taking your time," you say, "thank you for listening."

Instead of "sorry I'm emotional," you say these matterss to me."
Instead of "sorry to bother you," you say, "I need support." This shift is not arrogant. It is restoration. God's love does not tolerate you.

It delights in you.

When you stop apologizing for existing, you reclaim space God already gave you. You stop negotiating your worth. You stop introducing yourself as an inconvenience. And slowly, you learn that presence does not require permission, it requires courage.

💊 Faith Prescription: Replacing Apology With Ownership

This prescription invites you to notice when you apologize unnecessarily and gently replace it with ownership or gratitude. Not to shame yourself, but to rewire the belief beneath the habit. Take this prescription daily by pausing before you apologize and asking: *Did I do something wrong, or am I afraid of being seen?*

🧬 Spiritual Vitamin: Permission To Exist Fully

This spiritual vitamin restores internal permission to take up space without guilt. God does not regret creating you. Take this truth daily until presence no longer feels like intrusion.

🕊 Holy Spirit Consult

Ask gently:

- Where do I apologize automatically?
- What am I afraid will happen if I don't?
- What would it feel like to exist without shrinking?

Listen without judgment.

🙏 Guided Prayer

"God, I confess that I learned to apologize for existing. I made myself small to avoid rejection. Heal the belief that my presence is a burden. Teach me how to take up space without fear. Remember that I am welcome—not tolerated. Amen."

📝 Journal Pages: Reclaiming Your Space

Write honestly:
- When do I apologize unnecessarily?

____

____

____

- What am I really trying to protect myself from?

- What would change if I believed I belonged?

You were never an interruption. You were always intentional. You are allowed to exist, fully.

Chapter 17:

YOU LEARNED TO BE "LOW MAINTENANCE" SO YOU WOULDN'T BE LEFT

SYMPTOM: Emotional Self-Rationing And The Fear Of Being "Too Much"

One of the most socially reinforced symptoms of invisibility trauma is the decision, often unconscious, to become "low maintenance." You pride yourself on not needing much. You don't complain. You don't ask for reassurance. You don't require follow-up. You don't expect consistency. You adapt. You adjust. You tolerate gaps in communication, affection, and presence because you've learned that expecting more puts relationships at risk.

This symptom forms when connection felt conditional. At some point, you noticed that when you needed more attention, more care, more emotional presence, people pulled back. They grew distant. They became overwhelmed. They disappeared. So, you adjusted your expectations downward. You told yourself you didn't need much anyway. You decided it was better to ask for less than to risk losing everything. Being "low maintenance" became your insurance policy.

You learned to regulate yourself so others wouldn't have to. You learned to manage disappointment quietly. You learned to accept crumbs without comment. You learned to interpret inconsistency as busyness rather than disinterest. And because this strategy kept people around, even if only partially, it felt successful. But success came at a cost.

Emotional self-rationing teaches you to shrink your needs to match what others are willing to give. You stop asking for clarity. You stop expecting follow-through. You stop requiring presence. You convince yourself that consistency is optional, that care is a bonus, that reliability is too much to ask. And slowly, you train yourself to survive on less than you deserve.

This symptom often hides behind maturity.

You tell yourself you're independent. Easygoing. Flexible. You say things like, "I don't need much," or "I'm not like that," when what you really mean is, *I learned not to ask.* You minimize your disappointment because acknowledging it feels risky. You swallow frustration because naming it might make you seem demanding. You lower the bar because you don't trust it to be met. Over time, this pattern reshapes your sense of worth.

You begin believing that needing more makes you unlovable. Those expectations are burdensome. That emotional presence is optional. You adjust yourself to fit what's offered rather than seeking what's healthy. And because you are adaptable, people rarely notice how much you're giving up staying connected.

This symptom also affects your relationship with God. You approach Him carefully. You keep prayers reasonable. You hesitate to ask boldly. You don't want to seem ungrateful or demanding. You learned that asking for more invites is disappointing, so you settle for what feels safe. But safety built on scarcity is not peace. It's Survival.

TEACHING: God Does Not Ask You To Shrink Your Needs To Keep Love

God never asked you to become less needy to remain loved. In fact, Scripture consistently affirms the opposite: God draws near to the needy, the dependent, the ones who ask boldly and often. Love, in God's economy, is not sustained by self-denial, it is sustained by truth.

This teaching reframes need as invitation rather than liability. God is not overwhelmed by your needs. He is not exhausted by your requests. He is not threatened by your desire for consistency, presence, and care. God does not ration love, and He does not expect you to either. Jesus never praised people for settling.

He honored those who asked persistently. He responded to those who refused to be silent. He did not shame need, He met it. God's love does not require you to be low maintenance to be kept. It is not fragile. It does not disappear when you ask for more. It does not retreat when you express longing. Love that requires self-rationing is not love; it is tolerance.

Healing begins when you allow yourself to admit that you need more than you pretended. That you wanted consistency. That you deserved follow-through. That your needs were never excessive, they were simply unmet.

You are not "too much." You were under-supported. God is not asking you to become demanding. He is asking you to become honest.

When you stop shrinking your needs to fit what others offer, you begin reclaiming dignity. You stop negotiating for scraps. You stop apologizing for wanting depth. You start trusting that love does not need to be rationed to survive. God's care does not diminish when you ask for more.

It multiplies.

🔗 Faith Prescription: Naming Needs Without Self-Negotiation

This prescription invites you to stop pre-adjusting your needs to avoid rejection. Naming needs without self-negotiation means you state what you need honestly, without minimizing, qualifying, or apologizing. Take this prescription daily by noticing when you downplay a need and choosing to name it instead.

🧬 Spiritual Vitamin: Abundance, Not Scarcity

This spiritual vitamin restores trust that love is not limited. God does not ask you to settle to stay connected. Take this truth daily until you stop treating care as scarce.

🕊 Holy Spirit Consult

Ask gently:

- Where have I lowered my needs to keep connection?
- What am I afraid would happen if I asked for more?
- What would it look like to trust love without rationing?

Listen without rushing to soften the answer.

🙏 Guided Prayer

"God, I confess that I learned to be low maintenance to stay. I shrank my needs to avoid being left. Heal the belief that asking for more is dangerous.

Teach me how to trust love that doesn't require self-denial. Restore dignity where scarcity took root. Amen."

📝 Journal Pages: Reclaiming What You Minimized

Write honestly and without editing:
- What needs did I learn to downplay?

____

____

____

____

- When did I decide I was asking for too much?

____

____

____

____

- What would change if I believed my needs were valid?

____

____

____

____

You were not asking for too much. You were asking the wrong people or asking in a season that couldn't hold you. Now, you are allowed to want more without fear.

PERSONAL NOTES

____

____

____

____

____

____

FINAL DISCHARGE SUMMARY

Unseen Was a Season, Not a Sentence

You were never unloved. You were being prepared out of sight.

You did not imagine the pain of being unseen. It was real. It shaped you. It taught you how to survive quietly, how to adapt without complaint, how to carry weight without acknowledgment. It trained your nervous system, your faith, your expectations, and your voice. Being unseen was not a misunderstanding, it was an experience. And it left marks. But it was never a verdict on your worth.

What you lived through was a season, not a sentence. A process, not a punishment. A hidden chapter, not the conclusion of your story. You were not overlooked by God while you were overlooked by people. You were not forgotten while you were waiting. You were not unloved while you were unseen. You were being formed in places where applause could not reach, and validation could not be corrupt.

There are things God builds in obscurity that cannot survive premature visibility. You learned endurance before exposure. You learned discernment before recognition. You learned identity before influence. You learned how to hear God without external affirmation. You learned how to stand when no one was clapping. You learned how to exist without permission. These were not accidents. They were preparations.

Unseen seasons strip performance out of faith. They separate calling from applause. They teach you who you are when no one is watching. And now, you are being discharged, not because nothing happened, but because something *was completed*. You are being released from the lie that invisibility meant insignificance. You are being released from the belief that love had to be earned through usefulness. You are released from the habit of shrinking, apologizing, rationing, and silencing yourself to survive. You are not leaving this clinic as someone who "got through it." You are leaving as someone who understands it.

You understand now that being unseen taught you how to see yourself clearly. You understand that silence did not mean absence. You understand that waiting did not mean rejection. You understand that God's love never depended on who noticed you. And most importantly, you understand that you do not have to live like someone still waiting to be chosen. You are no longer negotiating for belonging. You are no longer auditioning for worth. You are no longer apologizing for taking up space.

You are walking out with identity intact, voice restored, needs validated, and presence reclaimed.

Discharge does not mean the memory disappears. It means the memory no longer defines you. You may still remember what it felt like to be unseen, but it will no longer tell you who you are. It will no longer decide how much you ask for. It will no longer dictate how small you stay. It will no longer convince you to expect less than God promised.

Because now you know the truth: You were never unloved. You were never forgotten. You were never overlooked by heaven. You were being prepared out of sight. And when God prepares something out of sight, it's because what's coming requires roots deep enough to stand without applause, identity strong enough to survive visibility, and faith solid enough to remain whole when the lights finally turn on.
You are discharged not to noise, but to confidence. Not into proving, but into presence. Not into striving, but into freedom. Go live like someone who knows they were never invisible to God.

Epilogue

Seen At Last, Starting With Yourself

This book was never about convincing the world to notice you. It was about teaching you how to stop disappearing in response to the world's silence. Being unseen shaped you, yes, but it does not get to define you. What once felt like neglect is now revealed as formation. What once felt like abandonment is now understood as preparation. And what once felt like invisibility is now recognized as a season where God was doing His most precise work, out of sight, but never out of reach.

You are not walking away from this journey as someone who "finally got noticed." You are walking away as someone who no longer needs to be. That is the deepest healing of all. When you stop measuring your worth by response, attention, or affirmation, you become unshakable. You are no longer vulnerable to the moods of rooms that don't know how to hold you. You are no longer dependent on recognition to feel real. You are real because God made you so, long before anyone acknowledged it.

The unseen season taught you things visibility never could. It taught you how to listen without external noise. It taught you how to trust God without confirmation. It taught you how to develop roots instead of chasing spotlight. Those lessons did not make you smaller; they made you steadier. They gave you a depth that does not evaporate when circumstances change. They gave you a faith that is not fragile, a voice that does not require permission, and an identity that does not need reinforcement to remain intact.

From this place forward, you get to live differently. You get to take up space without apology. You get to ask for what you need without minimizing it. You get to let yourself be known without fear of disappearance. You get to receive love without earning it, rest without guilt, and presence without performance. You are no longer living like someone trying to survive being overlooked. You are living as someone who knows exactly who they are, even if others are still catching up.

There will be moments when old reflexes try to return. Moments when silence feels personal. Moments when being unseen tempts you to shrink again. When that happens, remember this truth: healing does not mean the memory is gone; it means the memory no longer has authority. You are allowed to notice those moments without obeying them. You are allowed to feel them without being ruled by them. You are allowed to choose wholeness even when familiarity tries to pull you back into hiding.

This is not the end of your story. It is the end of one interpretation of it. The chapter where invisibility meant insignificance is closed. The chapter where silence meant rejection is finished. The chapter where survival required self-erasure is complete. What comes next is not louder, it is truer. Not flashier, steadier. Not performative rooted.

You are seen. You know. You are held. And not because the world finally noticed, but because you finally stopped disappearing. Go forward living like someone who knows the difference between being unseen and being unloved. You were never the same thing. And now, you never will be.

144

ABOUT THE AUTHOR

Dr. Patricia Tanner was born and raised in Sanford FL. She comes from a family of three siblings. Patricia Tanner is the founder of Multhai International Realty, Multhai Asset Management Services, and Multhai Investment Group which is located in Sanford, Florida. She is a graduate of the University of Central Florida, where she received a Bachelor of Science in Business Administration and a minor in Human Resources Management.

Dr. Tanner began her career shortly thereafter as a Regional Property Manager in the apartment community. Throughout her career in property management, she has built interpersonal relationships with corporate clients. She has a successful track record of increasing company revenues over $5 million annually, through hard work, commitment, creativeness, and strategic planning.

Her experience and leadership role eventually led her to achieve a Florida Real Estate Broker license. She spent fifteen years in the Real Estate field while completing a Master of Arts in Human Resources Management from Webster University, and a Master of Public Administration from Troy University. It was in this capacity that she decided to open her own brokerage company, Multhai International Realty.

In addition, Dr. Tanner finds time in her busy schedule to participate in her own Non-For-Profit Organization, Stones 2 Homes. She remains President of her organization in which she helps people build, keep, or purchase homes in affordable communities. She is the founder of PNT Property Partners in which she buys vacant land, develops it, and constructs brand new construction homes in Sanford Florida. Her overall goal is to educate and provide resources to help people overcome financial hardships and credit disadvantage to live the American Dream through homeownership in spite of economic hardship. Through her visions she will continue to grow as an entrepreneur and is willing to share her knowledge, experience, and expertise with anyone who is willing to learn.

MORE BOOKS BY THE AUTHOR

Welcome to the Faith Clinic—where your soul doesn't need to be perfect to be healed.

You've smiled through burnout. Quoted scripture while quietly unraveling. Prayed, fasted, and still felt like your faith flatlined. If that's you, Faith Clinic: Volume I is your spiritual prescription.

Dr. Patricia S. Tanner—known as The Faith Doctor—invites you into a raw, grace-filled recovery journey for the soul. With 7 powerful doses of faith-infused wisdom, this book delivers healing where performance failed and offers truth where church hurt left a scar. Designed especially for spiritually exhausted youth and young adults, each "dose" reads like an IV drip of hope for believers secretly running on empty.

You don't need to be okay to show up. You just need to be willing. The clinic is open.

NOW AVAILABLE:
www.amazon.com

Healing was just the beginning. Now it's time to grow.

If Faith Clinic Volume I met you in crisis, Volume II meets you in recovery. Because faith isn't a one-time fix—it's a lifestyle that needs maintenance, accountability, and consistency. Welcome to your follow-up care plan.

In Faith Clinic: Volume II, Dr. Patricia S. Tanner—aka The Faith Doctor—guides you through the next level of your spiritual healing journey. From navigating church trauma and burnout to facing silence from God and rediscovering purpose, this book goes deeper than devotionals. It's not about hype—it's about habits that sustain real, lasting transformation.

With raw wisdom, relatable stories, and no-shame truths, each chapter is a spiritual check-in for believers who want to thrive—not just survive. Whether you're wrestling with doubt, craving stability, or simply ready to grow up in God, this clinic is for you.

You've detoxed. Now it's time to build. Let's get you discharge ready.

NOW AVAILABLE:

www.amazon.com

Welcome to the Faith Clinic: Anxiety Edition — where God doesn't coddle your coping mechanisms but confronts them with surgical precision.

This book is for the ones who love Jesus but still can't sleep. For the worship leaders crying in church bathrooms. For the believers who pray in spirals, fight shame on Sundays, and secretly think, "Maybe I'm the only one who can't seem to breathe through this." You're not crazy. You're just in a fight — and this book is your spiritual triage.

Inside you'll find:
- Panic attacks in pews and the prayers that still work.
- Scriptures that talk you off the ledge.
- What to do when you feel numb and God feels quiet.
- How to walk out of shame loops, judgment spirals, and performance religion.

This isn't just encouragement. It's equipment.
Because healing isn't a moment — it's a walk.

NOW AVAILABLE:

www.amazon.com

Welcome to the Faith Clinic: Stress Edition — where we don't hand you cute verses and clichés. We hand you spiritual prescriptions for real pressure, real panic, and real prayers from tired believers holding it together by a thread.

This book is for the overwhelmed—those trusting God while juggling bills, burnout, hustle culture, and holy frustration. If you've ever whispered, "God, are You even watching this mess?" this is for you.

Inside you'll find raw, soul-hitting chapters like:

- "God, I Trust You — But These Bills Keep Coming"
- "If Rest Is Holy, Why Does It Feel Like Slacking?"
- "I'm Tired of Smiling So You Won't Worry"

This isn't fluff. It's real talk for real stress—and a reminder that you're not forgotten, you're being fortified.

The Faith Clinic is open. Breathe in & take your spiritual vitamins. Healing begins here.

NOW AVAILABLE:
www.amazon.com

This isn't just a feeling — it's a flare signal from the soul. You pray, serve, and believe in God, but something deep inside is still simmering. Welcome to the Faith Clinic: Anger Edition — where suppressed emotions meet sacred intervention.

In this volume, Dr. Patricia S. Tanner guides you through spiritual triage for:

- Silent rage and emotional suppression

- The grief–anger connection

- Rejection wounds from childhood to church hurt

This isn't a lecture. It's a spiritual detox. No shame. No sugar-coating. Just raw, honest healing. Whether you're snapping at loved ones or silently seething under the surface, this book meets you at the boiling point—and leads you to the breakthrough.

This is the clinic.

This is your moment.

And God is ready to heal the anger behind your amen.

NOW AVAILABLE:

www.amazon.com

In this powerful installment of the Faith Clinic series, Dr. Patricia S. Tanner brings biblical insight, emotional compassion, and spiritual strength to those walking through grief. Designed as a healing chamber for the soul, each "dose" of this devotional targets a different dimension of sorrow—guiding you from pain to peace, from mourning to joy.

Inside, you'll discover:

- Daily doses of Scripture-based encouragement.
- Personal reflections and prayers for each stage of grief.
- Practical faith prescriptions to help you process loss and find purpose.

Whether you are navigating the recent loss of a loved one, confronting buried grief from the past, or supporting someone else in their sorrow, this devotional offers a gentle yet powerful roadmap to healing. Come, take your seat in the Faith Clinic—where the Great Physician is ready to restore your soul.

NOW AVAILABLE:

www.amazon.com

30 Days Of Grieving

Given By The Inspiration Of God

Healing From COVID-19

Almost a year later, it hit me... My mother was gone, and I was still stuck at the hospital. I had tried everything from crying to counseling, and even prayer. Pray they told me. Trust God they insisted. But it seemed as if nothing was working. I was hurt, dealing with my reality: my mother was not coming back.

While journeying through grief, it was under the divine 'Inspiration of God' that He placed me in a trance. While I was gaining a revelation about grief, He gave me this journal, '30 Days Of Grieving.'

NOW AVAILABLE:
www.amazon.com

The 30 Days Challenge:

I Tested POSITIVE for COVID-19

If you had 30 days to live, what would you do? If you were told that you needed to prepare for a marathon in 30 days and you were completely out of shape, what would you do first? If a family member handed you one million dollars and told you that you had to figure out how to build a house (debt free), how would you execute your plan?

I'm catching you off guard with these requests, right? Well, this is exactly what COVID-19 did when it snatched my mother's life away, wrecking my entire world. I had to battle for my mother AND my faith in 30 days flat. What a challenge!

Throughout this book, I will walk you through my brief journey with COVID-19, negative of a happy ending. I will share the diary I kept while attending to my mother, and the scriptures I read, prayed, and quoted as my shield and protection.

Take the journey with me, there is healing on the other side!

NOW AVAILABLE:

www.amazon.com

Can Salvation Get You Into Heaven? The Answer Is Yes! offers a powerful and biblically grounded exploration of God's eternal plan, revealing the heart of the Gospel and the assurance of salvation through Jesus Christ.

 Unpacking life's most vital questions—Who is God? Why were we created? What does Jesus' life mean for us?—this book brings clarity to the believer's journey and confirms that salvation, once received, is eternally secure.

Whether you're seeking understanding or affirming your faith, this inspiring guide will lead you into the confidence and joy of knowing heaven is your eternal home.

NOW AVAILABLE:
www.amazon.com

The Bench That Waited is a bold and prophetic call to action for believers who've grown comfortable in church attendance but stagnant in purpose.

With raw honesty and spiritual insight, Patricia Tanner exposes the quiet crisis of passive faith—where callings are delayed and obedience is optional.

Through Scripture, stories, and reflection, this book urges readers to rise from routine, break free from spiritual stagnation, and step boldly into their Kingdom assignment. The bench has waited long enough—will you?

NOW AVAILABLE:
www.amazon.com

What happens when the Kingdom becomes a stranger?

The Godless Climb is not a rejection of faith—it is a raw, unflinching journey through what remains when belief unravels. With brutal honesty and tender grace, this book explores the spiritual free fall that follows the loss of divine certainty, the ache of unanswered prayers, and the void left when God no longer feels near.

Written for those who have quietly slipped out of the pews and into a wilderness of doubt, grief, and inner searching, this is not a triumph story—but a survival story. A confession. A sacred wrestle. Through personal reflection and prophetic insight, the author unpacks what it means to climb without a safety net, to live without the scaffolding of religious performance, and to build a new compass in the absence of old crutches.

You haven't arrived. But you're still climbing. And that is holy.

NOW AVAILABLE:

www.amazon.com

It Was The God In

Me

Success can be attributed to many things. Depending on the person who has obtained success would determine those to whom they attribute their success. Some give credit to their daily routine while others give credit to a mentor or some sort of system they followed. When I think about my success, the only person who I can give the credit to is God.

In this memoir, I share the successes and failures I have experienced throughout my life. From my individual experiences to my entrepreneurial journey, I share how God has walked with me every step of the way.

Come and see.. It Was The God In Me!!

NOW AVAILABLE:
www.amazon.com

The Triple 7 Formula is designed for business owners who are looking forward to hitting the million-dollar mark in their business. If you own a business and seem to be running in financial circles, this book will get you on track to simultaneously gaining sound business structure and millions in your bank account.

It was through many conversations with business owners lacking financial gain that prompted Patricia to share her blueprint for millionaire status. Through this book, she demonstrates how to gain financial ground by developing strong teams, implementing systems, and setting stackable goals. If you are ready to gain a laser sharp focus, and implement these clear steps, you will position yourself for financial greatness. Your business will be sound, and you will see financial growth beyond your wildest dreams!!

NOW AVAILABLE:

www.amazon.com

The Triple 7 Formula is specifically crafted for business owners aspiring to reach the million-dollar milestone. If you are a business owner feeling stuck in financial cycles, this book will set you on the path to building both a solid business structure and financial success.

This workbook is designed to complement the textbook of the same name. As you progress through its pages, you will be inspired to take decisive steps toward becoming a millionaire. From constructing your business framework to creating the millionaire's avatar, this process will expand your knowledge and mindset. Not only will you chart a course to financial success, but you will also identify your accountability circle and select a mentor to guide you toward greatness.

I cannot guarantee millionaire status unless you actively follow the steps to begin your journey. If you are searching for a get rich quick scheme, this workbook is not for you. I am looking for those ready to put in the effort—and since you are reading this, I believe that's you!

You have finally found it: Your roadmap to millions!

NOW AVAILABLE:
WWW.Amazon.com

Find Patricia on The Web:

www.PatriciaTanner.com

Follow Patricia on social media:

Facebook & Instagram: @PatriciaTannerInc

162

www.ingramcontent.com/pod-product-compliance
Lightning Source LLC
Chambersburg PA
CBHW071308030726
47594CB00002B/356